Trapping: A Practical Guide

TRAPPING: A Practical Guide

JAMES A. BATEMAN

STACKPOLE BOOKS

Published by
STACKPOLE BOOKS
Cameron and Kelker Streets
P.O. Box 1831
Harrisburg, Pa. 17105

Published simultaneously in Don Mills, Ontario, Canada
by Thomas Nelson & Sons, Ltd.

Library of Congress Cataloguing in Publication Data

Bateman, James A.
The trapper's guide.

Bibliography: p.
Includes index.
1. Trapping. I. Title.
SK283.B33 639'.1 78-15117
ISBN 0-8117-1743-7

PRINTED IN THE UNITED STATES OF AMERICA

Contents

Acknowledgements

Few non-fiction books are produced without help and advice coming to the author from a wide range of sources, and this one is no exception.

I have received a great deal of information from readers of my first book on this subject and included among these are: Lt. Col. Bruce Donald, Ronald Bowen, Peter Etheridge, A. G. Credland and Monica Ganter.

I am grateful for information supplied by the Division of Wildlife Services, US Department of the Interior, concerning legislation for trapping in the United States.

I have also received information concerning the traps currently being marketed by Gilbertson & Page Ltd, James Wood Products and A. D. Ltd.

Other than the use of photographs from the files of the Department of Zoology, National Museum of Wales, the work of Mr Erick Broadbent, I am indebted to the Forestry Commission, the Ministry of Agriculture Fisheries and Food, Philip Glasier and C. Howell for making photographs available to me.

I am particularly grateful to my wife for encouragement and forbearance at a time when writing the book was combined with a change in employment and home. She has also given generous assistance with proof-reading and the preparation of the index.

Introduction

Trapping Past

Was there ever a time when human beings could exist in isolation without the benefits derived from other animals, thus having no need to capture them? For a brief span our distant ancestors may have survived naked and as vegetarians. Before long, however, people moving northwards from the central regions of the earth, where it is believed man had his origin, must have met the southward-creeping ice-sheet. The unusual cold encountered could only have been tolerated by getting extra heat-producing foods inside the body and a warm covering on the outside.

Early men may have been more hairy than the woolliest of present-day folk, but comparing their natural insulation against the cold with the shaggy coats of a woolly rhinoceros or mammoth, they must have felt deprived. Little wonder that they sought ways and means to procure such coats for their own comfort, and when they had skinned an animal why should they waste the meat?

With little or nothing in the way of weapons it would be a natural thought to set traps, and the sight of large animals caught in naturally occurring pits would have provided an incentive. So it was that pitfall traps were first made by men and in the natural sequence of events they also developed rawhide snares, sometimes sprung with the aid of saplings.

Living close to nature, the early settlers of 10,000 years ago discovered other habits of animals which they could utilize to their advantage. Well-trodden paths through forests and grassland, the things we now call game-trails, were natural sites on which to set traps. The shores of lakes and the banks of waterholes might be ringed with thirsty animals in the early morning and just before dusk – what better time and place in which to set traps? But they would have to be set under water, and in the days before men discovered how to win metals from ores, they would need to use waterproof woods like oak and teak. An ability to withstand immersion in water also provided timber like oak with a quality for survival through time, and we can be grateful that this very ruggedness has preserved the oaken treadle-traps originally designed for catching deer at water-holes. These traps remained hidden in the beds of lakes and bogs for many centuries before rediscovery all over Europe during the past hundred years.

When trade became an established feature of human cultural development the value of animal skins for barter or sale was soon recognized. So the fur trade was born and with it a revolution in the design and manufacture of traps. Associated with this were advanced skills in siting and baiting traps, so that the commercial trapper achieved renown, not only as a resourceful businessman but also as a keenly observant naturalist, since knowing the habits of animals was an essential ingredient for success. Before long the local blacksmith was making the newly conceived iron and steel traps and when the demand for these overtook him small factories took over, sometimes making traps as a sideline but often as the sole product. The names of Duke, Waring, Crisp & Co and W. & G. Sidebotham in Britain, and Newhouse in North America became household words in the realm of trapping.

The influence of popular fashion created a boom in furs during the nineteenth and early twentieth centuries, but more recently this has been overtaken by the incensed feelings of a generation newly aware of nature conservation and cruelty to animals. Certainly, whether or not one condones trade in wild animals, which first requires that they are captured, it is an uncivilized person who accepts that capture and cruelty must needs go hand in hand.

This is a welcome state of affairs and a sign of human maturity. It has also imposed, either by desire or by legislation, a worldwide

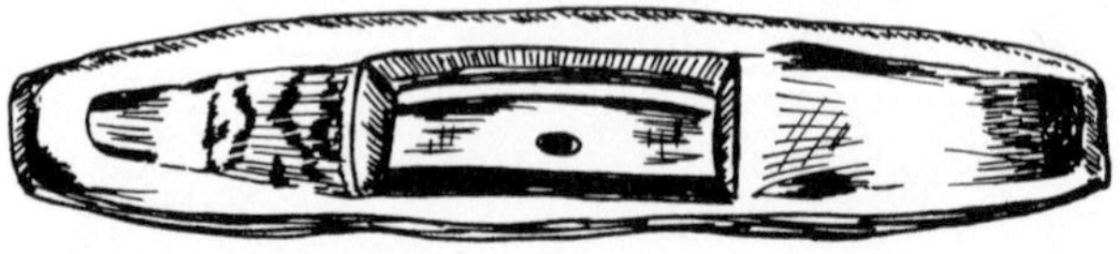

Fig 1 Wooden treadle trap from a peat bog

trend to replace vicious and cruel traps by humane counterparts. There are now societies in most countries intent either upon the abolition of fur-trading, or on ensuring human kindness towards animals.

Inevitably inefficient and illegal apparatus has become obsolete, and this in turn creates an antiquarian value. Trap collecting as a hobby seems to be increasing; indeed there may even be some opportunity for investment value. Certainly a Japanese clockwork fly-trap of early twentieth-century origin recently won a £100 prize for its owner in a hardware-trade competition for relics. There is also reference value in old catalogues, such as the recently re-issued 1917 catalogue of the Army and Navy Stores in London, which has several pages dealing with traps of the period.

How Traps Work

Whereas there are probably thousands of different designs for traps, some of which also come in a range of sizes appropriate to differently sized animals, from a functional point of view they can all be divided into relatively few types.

Pitfall Traps

These must have been the earliest forms of traps and the first to be used were unlikely to have been man-made, since the availability of natural pits and depressions in the ground, cavities among rocks and the beds of dried-up streams meant that they could have been used without human effort. Later, human ingenuity increased the efficiency of bare, empty pits with the art of camouflage and the use of lead-in pathways.

Catching an animal in a pit is one thing, killing it when its natural ferocity has been sharpened by capture is another. If luck was with the early hunters, an animal might break a leg when crashing down into a pit, but while this might hinder its movement and ability to escape, it might make it even fiercer. If trapping and killing could be combined, so much the better. So long pointed staves were driven into the ground at the bottom of the pits to impale the hapless creatures which fell into them. Variations of such traps are still being used by people living as primitive hunters and foragers in the undeveloped countries;

sometimes the pits are refined by lining them with timber or corrugated iron and the wooden staves are replaced by iron spikes.

At the other end of the scale, pitfall traps are now frequently used for catching insects, either to control pests or for purposes of scientific research. Glass jars buried in the ground with their mouths at soil level form ideal insect traps and if they are deep enough they can also catch small vermin.

Variations of pitfall traps have included the addition of a pivoted platform across the mouth, designed to tip an animal into the pit when stepped upon. Very deep pits have been filled with a fair depth of water to drown small animals that fall into them.

Adhesion Traps

Naturally occurring sticky surfaces were the other form of trap which would have been noticed by early men and in time inspired them. Resin exuding from tree trunks or honey dripping from a wild comb produce natural traps which combine a ready-made bait with a catching device for insects. It requires only a little more thought to evolve the manufacture of such traps from pieces of wood, metal or glass painted with a solution of boiled sugar.

Similarly, a very old method used for capturing wild birds that perch—one still used in some parts of the world—is to paint the branches of trees with bird lime, a concoction made by boiling wood chippings from holly or slippery elm until a sticky broth is formed.

Snares

Of all the traps devised by man, these must surely be the simplest and commonest. Though they have been readily available for purchase through hardware stores, they are still frequently home-made from all kinds of raw materials. The earliest forms were made from plant fibres, rawhide strip, dried animal sinews and horsehair, whereas more recently wire and synthetic cords have been used.

Known as 'wires' by countrymen in Britain, they combine all the virtues of an efficient trap—portability, simple operation and silent action—but unless they are very skilfully constructed with a stop to the slip-knot, which should use a brass eyelet hole for preference, and incorporate a swivel action, they are to be condemned; they can inflict too much suffering upon their victims. Nevertheless, they remain the poacher's supreme weapon, whether the catch is to be a rabbit or an elephant.

Spring Traps

The range here is colossal, from spring-loaded snares, where the spring may be nothing more than a bent sapling, to huge flat-sprung steel bear traps or coil-sprung jump traps.

The group can be subdivided into categories which include the so-called steel traps also known as leg-hold traps and in Britain as gin traps, the breakback or clap-traps used for capturing rats and mice, pincer traps for taking moles in their underground runs and the humane traps which are meant to kill rather than immobilize and maim animals.

Spring traps depend upon a triggering device which releases the spring tension, and this may also double as a bait pan. When released from tension the spring activates one or a pair of jaws which snap around a foot, the head or the middle of the body.

Some early attempts at transforming inhumane steel traps included covering the jaws with rubber, to hold an animal without hurting it. Considering the inherent power of the springs and the fact that an animal is unlikely to rest quietly in the trap without attempting to wrench itself free, they cannot have been a success.

Foot Traps

Apart from using steel leg-hold traps, which might well be included here, there are other ways of securing an animal by its foot in a trap. The wheel trap used in Africa for catching giraffes or antelopes consists of a wheel of plaited grass from the rim of

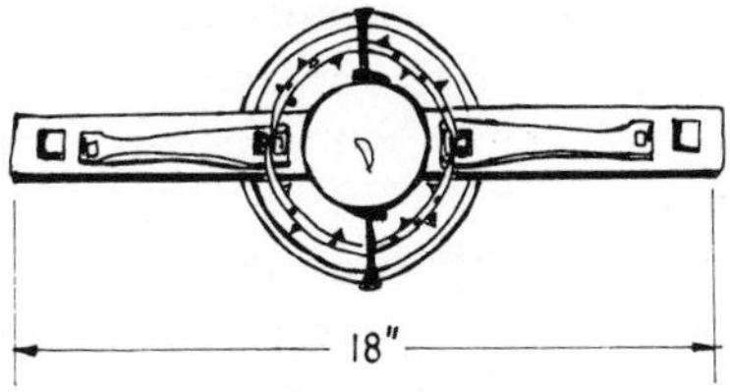

Fig 2 A sixteenth-century iron leg-hold trap

which are fastened centre-pointing sharpened staves of wood or metal. Anchored over a depression in a game path, the animal is taken when its foot is pushed through the 'spokes'. The treadle traps mentioned earlier for use under water were also foot traps, although they had a spring element to release the gripping wooden jaws.

Cage Traps

This is a general term to describe what are often referred to as live traps. The body of the cage may consist of metal rods or wire bars, wire mesh or simply solid walls of wood or metal. There are frequently entrances at opposite ends, although some traps have only a single entrance. In either case the objective is to induce an animal to enter the cage, and then to activate some triggering device which will close the doors with the victim inside. The inducement is usually some kind of bait, on which the success of these traps largely depends, with due exploitation of the natural curiosity of many animals.

Cage traps can be of all sizes, from those designed specifically for shrews and mice to enormous, heavily built constructions for big jungle cats. They can be used for taking most kinds of animals as well as fish and birds. The lobster pot, or creel, is a good example. Cage traps are not always automatic, some relying upon the captive animal to trigger the closing mechanism; the simplest depend upon a hidden trapper pulling a release cord to close the door once the animal is safely inside.

As the description 'live traps' suggests, their virtue is in preventing injury and suffering to their captives, although it must be stressed that fairly constant inspection is necessary if animals are not to suffer from lack of food or exposure to heat and cold. There is, of course, the problem of killing trapped animals, if this is the ultimate purpose of the exercise, and it may be difficult to get an animal out of a trap if it is any way fierce. The point of using a live trap if the animal is going to be killed anyway is that there is then a choice and an opportunity to do the job humanely. An even greater advantage is that no animal need be killed unintentionally. In the past numerous pet dogs and cats, as well as harmless creatures of the field, were victims of steel traps that could hardly ever be used selectively.

Elaborate Traps

Traps of some considerable size or particularly complicated mechanism are relatively few in number but are interesting because of their mode of operation.

Springing immediately to mind is the kind of fish trap used in river estuaries or in bays, consisting essentially of a series of boom nets which channel fish into the trap net. A similar device on dry land can be used to herd game animals, such as antelopes, into a catch-pen.

Lights or radiant energy can be employed to attract insects. These can be incorporated into a netting funnel construction or combined with an electrically driven fan to propel the insects into a well containing a killing fluid.

Do-it-Yourself Traps

While many of the traps are made by enthusiasts possessing a handyman turn of mind, there are many that can be made on the trail from whatever comes to hand—brushwood, vegetable fibres and rocks. Backwoodsmen, poachers, nomadic tribesmen and boy scouts have all tried their hand at this, some as an everyday chore to provide something for the pot. Chapter 5 shows that this trap lore is an important feature of survival training for the armed forces of many countries.

Included here is the deadfall trap, which releases a heavy weight in the form of a rock or log when a simple trigger is activated. A primitive but effective variation of the deadfall trap can be traced back to Roman times: this is to saw most of the way through a tree trunk known to be a scratching post for heavy animals so that when they come along to scratch, the trunk gives way and topples over to kill them.

Uses of Traps

Originally employed for protection against wild creatures—perhaps a series of pits in front of a cave dwelling—or to provide a supply of meat and fur wraps, it is necessary to point out that trapping is still part of the daily life of people in the undeveloped areas of the world.

The same basic purpose of trapping can be expanded in

order to build up an industry, such as fishing with salmon traps or lobster pots.

The problem of controlling large predatory animals may have disappeared for most of us, but there are still plenty of smaller animals which farmers and gamekeepers are only too anxious to keep under control. While it is possible to shoot them, this is time consuming and so it is often more desirable to let a line of traps do the job while you are warmly tucked up in bed. There are also poisons which can be used to get rid of vermin, but they are difficult to use in isolation so that there is no danger to domestic or harmless wild animals.

Increasingly, scientists are turning to traps in their research programmes, not to eradicate animals, although sometimes they are concerned with pest control, but to capture them on a large scale from a particular area of land with a minimum of effort. In this way it is possible to conduct sample population surveys to a pattern that can be repeated and so avoid criticism of using variable techniques which provide a discrepancy in the final results.

Finally in this introduction, it is a duty to stress the care which must be observed in using traps, especially to ensure that as far as is humanly possible traps are so set and sited that they take only the creatures for which they are being employed. It is similarly necessary to appreciate the potential suffering of animals if traps are not used sensitively and skilfully. It is not always easy to establish the kind of pain and suffering that an animal feels, but it must be a fact that animals with reasonably complex nervous systems must feel the same kind of pain that we experience when injured. In many of the higher animals, our own domestic pets for example, it is possible to see from the expression on their faces when they are in pain and some of them will let us know in a much more positive way when they are unhappy with life.

Whenever there is legislation which affects or controls the use of traps or trapping procedures, this will be explained. Anyone who contemplates using traps to capture animals must be quite sure of the legal situation in the district where the trapping is to take place.

1 Trapping Mammals

The fur-bearing animals of the world are mammals and this fact alone suggests a special reason for wanting to trap them.

Apart from the value of the flesh as a source of food, the fat for lubrication, insulation and even as fuel for illumination, and horns, antlers and claws as weapons or tools, the value of fur as a body covering or for furnishing dwelling places goes back into prehistory.

Trapping has for long been the favoured means of catching fur-bearing mammals and this is understandable when it is appreciated how much damage can be caused to a pelt by spear thrusts or by bullets—not that traps always prevent damage: because of this there have been many attempts to invent traps that will kill without causing harm to the skins.

Another factor must be taken into account when devising mammal traps. These animals have the best developed brains in the animal kingdom; they certainly display intelligence which cannot be readily associated with other animals, even with birds. There is considerable variation in the grades of intelligence and this must be taken into account when traps are being designed and even more so when they are being sited. Mammal intelligence plays an important part in protecting these animals and it is variously aided by different forms of environmental awareness from the use of ears, eyes and a sense of smell.

Few mammals use all of these senses equally well or simultaneously. In most individual types it is one or other of these faculties which is used predominantly. Thus animals which are preyed upon, a group which includes most of the herbivores—the vegetation feeders—tend to have acute vision and often a keen sense of hearing. The predators, often hunting at night or in the early morning and evening, find that at a distance their sight is less useful for detecting their prey, so they rely upon hearing slight sounds and, more frequently, smelling familiar scents to alert them.

This knowledge can be most useful when setting out to trap mammals. Animals with good vision have an awareness of slight changes within their immediate environment, particularly the sudden appearance of something different and strange. Animals depending upon sight to alert them seldom rush headlong into danger, unless of course they are being chased, so they are not likely to be taken in traps set crudely and without any attempt at camouflage.

Animals which rely upon their sense of smell often possess an extensive awareness of individual smells, either for warning them of the presence of enemies or in order to whet their appetites. For most mammals other than the domestic species, the smell of man gives rise to immediate caution and frequently fear. For this reason, great care must be taken to ensure that human smell is not associated with traps. Some animals, such as rats, are deterred by the smell of the blood of their own kind, so traps must be cleaned when traces of blood from previous catches have soiled them. Alternatively, smells of natural surroundings arouse no suspicion and this can be used to advantage by ensuring that new traps are 'seasoned' before being used, by placing them out-of-doors to capture the smell of nature. They can be buried in soil, left in a pond or covered for a while with vegetation.

Trapping and Commerce

Fur-trapping is a commercial enterprise and in the past it has played an important part in the economy of a number of countries, especially Canada, the United States, Russia and former colonial governments in Africa, Asia and South America.

A number of developments in recent years have caused a reduction in the size of this enterprise, not the least being a widespread movement to discourage trading in the pelts of wild animals, particularly in the fashion trade. An increase in the ranching of fur-bearers has been accompanied by the greater availability of, and a liking for, simulated furs produced by manufacturers from man-made fibres. The development of the synthetic fibres industry has played a large part in freeing man of the need to kill animals for their fur. Apart from the dictates of fashion, furs were often essential in past years to provide warmth during conditions of extreme cold, such as arctic and antarctic exploration and mountaineering. Now the use of nylon and other fibres in the manufacture of waterproof and insulated clothing has replaced the need for furs.

Pest Control

Trapping mammals for their fur appears to be on the decline; meanwhile there is little to suggest that the activities of mammalian pests are undergoing a similar decline and there are constant reports of the nuisance of foxes, stoats, weasels, rats and mice in Britain and Europe. In North America a similar nuisance is caused by coyotes, skunks, racoons, lynxes and gophers, to name a few. In some countries killing pests is regarded as a legitimate exercise for which there are no restrictions, so that the types of traps used, the places in which they are put down and the ways of setting them are not controlled in any way. Elsewhere, in Britain, New Zealand and certain of the United States, for example, the steel trap is banned, even for taking pests. To replace them for the purposes of exterminating vermin, a general and collective name often used for mammalian pests, so-called humane traps have been produced. Like the steel or leg-hold traps, the replacements are spring powered, but are meant to kill instantly by a blow on the head or body. Often the use of these traps is further safeguarded by legal requirements concerning the way they are set and the conditions for placing them at a site.

In some countries the animals considered to be pests are listed and elsewhere the use of traps is often licensed, with traps numbered for registration purposes.

Research

There are many occasions when scientists need to monitor wildlife populations. This may be in order to assess population fluctuations related either to seasonal or climatic changes, or in response to changes within an environment in which they are found. Mammals can be vectors (carriers) of parasites such as tapeworms, flukes, mites, ticks and fleas, some of which might be disease agents affecting man and his domestic stock. It is desirable in these cirumstances to catch samples for investigation. Sometimes it is also essential for scientists to study wild animals under laboratory conditions in order to investigate feeding habits, breeding processes, aspects of behaviour and even the way that they move about.

For most scientific purposes wild animals are needed alive and for this special kinds of traps are employed. These are variously described as live traps, box traps and cage traps. They are often quite small, suitable for capturing the junior grades of rodents, or relatively strong and giant-sized for foxes or even larger mammals. Very often the captives are examined in the field and then released, so that the interference with their lives is minimal. Sometimes marking devices are used, such as fur-dyeing, shaving, ear-clipping and tattooing, to provide a means of recognizing animals recaptured on a later occasion and for furnishing evidence of the range of their movements.

Bats are flying mammals and are often difficult to catch as they roost in places often providing little means of access, such as church towers and the lofts of buildings. To make the task easier, scientists have been using mist nets with some success in recent years. The techniques used are the same as those described for capturing birds (see Chapter 2).

Spring and Steel Traps

The trap which in North America has, for over a century, been known as the steel trap, has in Britain been known as the gin trap. The word 'gin' is presumably a corruption of engine, because all kinds of traps have been known as engines and the term is obviously appropriate when there is a spring-motivated action. Especially in the United States and Canada these traps have also been known as leg-hold traps, because it is usually around the leg that the trap jaws snap. This results in what can only be excruciating pain for the animals captured and unless the traps are inspected regularly such pain might have to be endured for a long period of time. It has always been understood by professional trappers that their traps should be inspected, but when a trap line may stretch for a mile (1.6km) or more it is easy to see how some traps may be overlooked.

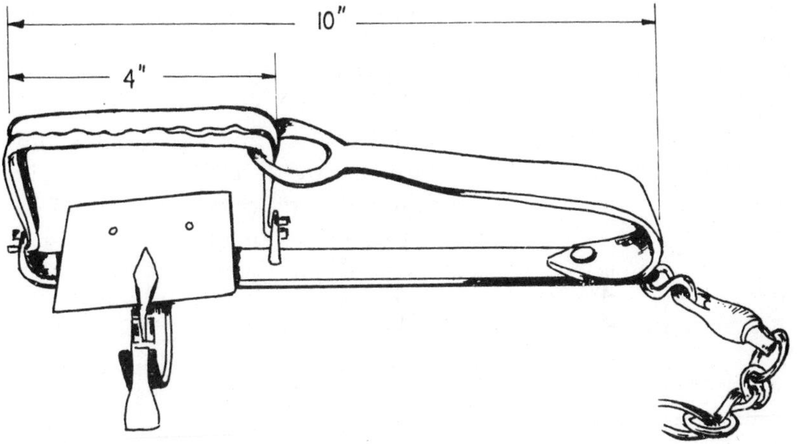

Fig 3a Sprung steel trap

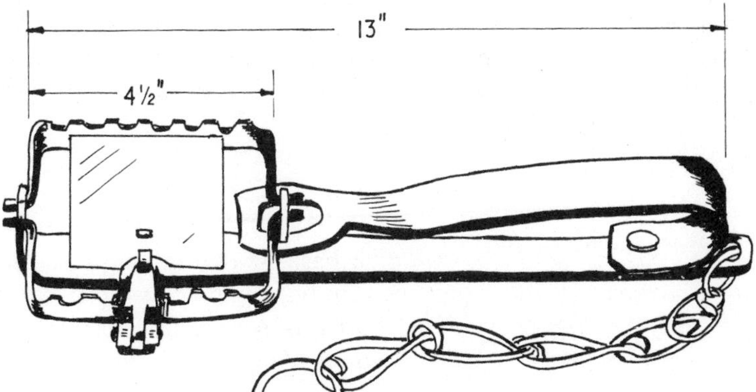

Fig 3b Set steel trap

Because many of these traps are still around and potentially lethal, it is as well to know something about them. There are many countries where they are still not illegal. A basic pattern is seen in Figure 3. It consists of a flat baseplate which may or may not be curved over at one end to form a continuous spring. In the example illustrated the spring is a separate piece of steel which is riveted to one end of the base. The other end of the baseplate is turned up to provide an eye inside which the ends of the jaws can rotate. At a distance equal to the width of the jaws from the end of the baseplate there is another eyed-plate to take the other end of the jaws. The end of the spring also has an eye and this fits over the last-mentioned eyed-plate. The spring has to be depressed in order that the jaws can open (Figure 3b). On the baseplate and between the jaws a pan is pivoted and this may or may not be baited. Projecting outwards from the baseplate and under the pan is the trigger bar or shank and the trigger, or dog, is hinged to the outer end. With the jaws open and flat on either side of the pan, the trigger is hinged over one jaw and caught on the edge of the pan. The trap usually has a chain or wire attached to the end of the baseplate so that it can be anchored.

There are numerous variations of this basic pattern, but the main one is where there are two springs, one eyed to each side of the jaws (Figure 4).

While many experienced trappers claim that steel traps can be used so that they will take only the animals for which they have been set, such declarations must be taken with considerable suspicion. Certainly some trappers have proved themselves so expert in knowing the habits of animals that their choice of trap

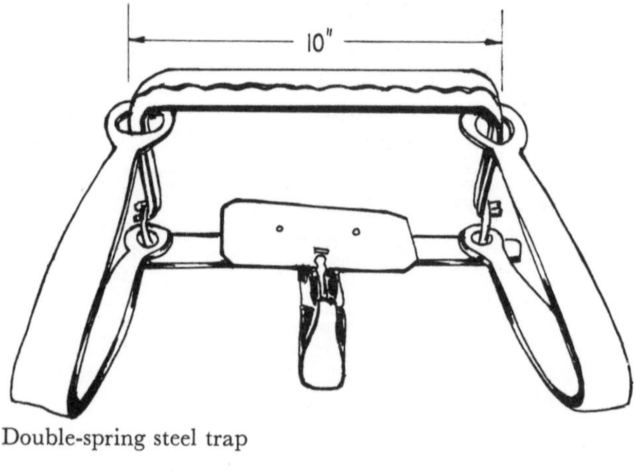

Fig 4 Double-spring steel trap

and the method of setting it can ensure an almost 99 per cent chance of capturing the animal for which it has been set. Even so, there can be no guarantee that animals will not suffer.

There is often a further unpleasant sequel to an animal being caught in a leg-hold trap. The ordinary version seldom closes on the higher and fleshier portion of a leg, but more usually around the foot. Here the bones have little muscular padding so that a struggling animal can quickly chafe away the flesh to bare the bones. Even worse, either by twisting the foot or by biting, the bone can be broken and the foot amputated. In this way animals often escape, but remain lame thereafter, or they die through septic infection of the wound.

Jump traps are available, which spring up when an animal is taken. The jaws are released higher up on the leg and so prevent 'wringing' or 'wringing off' to use the terms which are employed for the amputation process. Similarly, a stop-loss trap incorporates an additional guard which holds the body and prevents an animal from gnawing itself.

There have been attempts to convert steel traps of the leg-hold type into humane forms. The usual steel trap, certainly most of those in use in the United States, have toothed jaws. Sometimes the teeth are not much more than wavy lines which interlock the two jaws. More often they are deep serrations which interlock with a grip from which escape, other than by amputation, is impossible. There were British-made traps that had toothless jaws and while these caused less immediate damage to the flesh, the grip was, none the less, very tight and escape unlikely.

In the United States, teeth have sometimes been filed off the jaws and these have been wrapped around with weatherstripping (draught-proofing sealing strip). The impact of trap jaws treated in this way is far less than with conventional jaws and a US Assistant Secretary of the Interior has reported that in experiments with modified versions one coyote was recaptured sixteen times without suffering injury. The extent of mental suffering is difficult to verify, but it is inconceivable that there would be none.

Also in the United States there has been limited use of poison or tranquillizer tabs attached to the traps. As originally used by the Fish and Wildlife Service, they consisted of strychnine wrapped in a paraffin-dipped rag, and while death would be relatively quick, when caused by strychnine it would also be very painful, so one would hesitate to use this technique.

The tranquillizer form used Diazepam, a member of the Valium group of drugs. The method employed was to sprinkle the drug into petroleum jelly (Vaseline) which is spread on a piece of rotted cloth. This, in turn, is rolled up and dipped in a paste made of beeswax and paraffin. The whole tab is wired to a trap jaw. The dose can be varied according to the animal likely to be caught, one gram being enough for a coyote and half of this for a fox. When animals are caught they will tear at the tab and the swallowed drug will induce drowsiness within half an hour and be effective for several days. The advantage of this, if steel traps are being used, is to prevent damage to limbs beyond that caused by the initial impact of the jaws. Writhing and consequent wringing will not occur. In cold conditions animals will quickly freeze to death after taking the drug. It should be noted that this drug is not generally available and some negotiation may be necessary where its use is contemplated.

Sets used with Leg-hold Traps

Trail-Sets

The most commonly employed set is the one known as the trail-set. This is used where animals are habitual followers of a particular route, which can be detected by wear on the vegetation through which they travel. The path is often called a run.

Among mammals which make runs are voles and gophers, in these cases quite diminutive and often in shrub and scrub. Rabbits also create runs in grassland and woodland, while badgers frequent the woods and also heaths. Otter and beaver runs will be found alongside water, and rats make obvious runs in farm buildings, especially grain stores. The nature of rat runs in buildings would not, however, favour the use of a trail-set.

When a trail-set is to be used, the ground is hollowed out to take the shape of the trap with its jaws open and deep enough for it to be just below the surface (see Figure 5). The trap is placed in the hollow and the jaws opened, care being taken to ensure that they have freedom of movement and that the ground will not cave in over them. The trap must be anchored and when it is

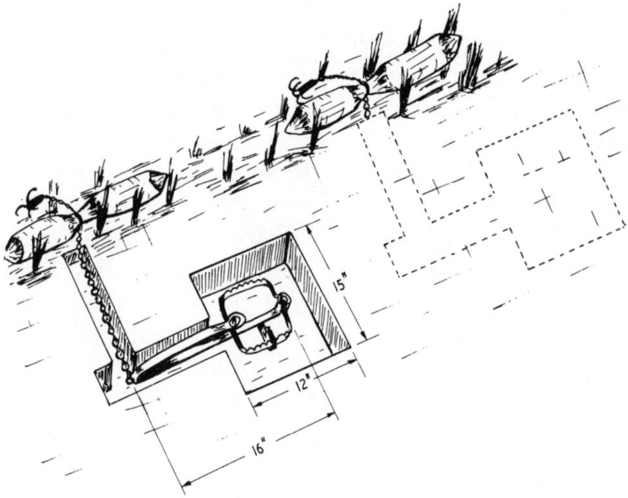

Fig 5 Trail-set with traps and clogs

only small this can be done by fastening a long staple over the baseplate and pinning it to the ground. With a large trap a clog is needed. A clog is a log which has a waist cut around its middle and the trap chain is attached to this. The clog also has a trap-drag or grappling hook to prevent it from being dragged away. A drag can easily be made from a piece of lead piping through the end of which three or four long nails are hammered; then the piping is flattened and the nail points bent over to form claws.

The trap pan and jaws are covered over with a piece of paper so that the soil used to cover the trap does not foul the mechanism. The soil should be sieved as finely as possible and after the trap is covered should be brushed over to give as natural an appearance as is feasible. Trappers often set clusters of traps in this manner along a trail, so that should an animal fail to step on one, it would be extremely lucky to avoid the others. When traps are set in this way no bait is used because it is intended that an animal will be caught by putting its foot on the buried pan. Knowing the gait of a particular animal and the distance apart of its feet when walking and running is useful when deciding the intervals of the traps in a cluster.

Drowning Sets

This is a way of using leg-hold traps for taking aquatic mammals such as otters, mink, beavers and muskrats. The traps are set alongside water in situations where water-living animals are likely to be found. They can be set in a similar manner to the trail-set, except that in this case the use of a bait may be valuable —fish would be ideal. If the trap is buried, the fish can be suspended from a pole over the trap. The animal will jump up and down and try to grasp the bait, and in so doing it is most likely to step on the buried pan, tripping the trigger. Drowning sets depend for their success in being sited at the edge of deep water; a shelving bank is not satisfactory, it must be steep. The reason for this is that a water animal when trapped will immediately dive into the water. To ensure that it is drowned the trap must have a sufficiently heavy weight attached so that when the animal enters the water the weight pulls it down and keeps it under. In this set, although the trap is weighted, it must have a length of wire or chain sufficient to reach the bottom of the water, and should be anchored to a clog so that it is not carried away in deep water and therefore difficult to retrieve.

It is important to realize that while this set has some humane aspects, because the trapped animal is certain to die from drowning and it is unlikely that wringing off will occur, the time taken for a water animal to drown is not short. For a beaver it could be anything up to twenty minutes.

Bait Sets

These are, in principle, very like the trail-set and the drowning set. The trap is buried with exactly the same procedure as in the trail-set, but bait is used as in the drowning set. Of course, traps are not placed near to water, because they are not meant for aquatic animals. The purpose is to catch mammals which have less well-defined trails—the kind like foxes, for example, which tend to follow their noses or move in response to sounds.

For such animals the bait is chosen appropriately, so that for a fox a freshly killed bird would be attractive. It is usual, as with the drowning set, to swing the bait over the trap from a pole, the height being adjusted so that it is just out of reach of the animal for which the trap has been set. This encourages the animal to jump up and down and so eventually step on the pan. It works with most members of the dog family, including wolves, jackals and wild hunting dogs. Incidentally, for these animals it pays to place sticks either side of the trap as a lead-in over the surface under which the trap is buried.

An alternative to using an edible bait, and one especially useful for catching wild cats which are inquisitive, is to substitute a bundle of feathers or even a bird's wing as the bait on the end of the pole. The movement in a breeze will attract the attention of cats which find such curiosities irresistible and will jump up and down in an attempt to get at them.

When considering the use of baits in conjunction with leg-hold traps, it must be understood that bait is never placed on the trap pan. These traps are intended to catch hold of the leg, whereas by placing bait on the pan there would be a chance of animals being caught by their mouths.

For catching underground moving mammals—the group that includes stoats, weasels and similar vermin—a trap set known as the Idstone can be very successful. It depends for its success upon the curiosity of these animals, their keen sense of smell and the readiness with which under natural conditions they will move through land drains. The set is constructed as seen in Figure 6. A hole about 15in (380mm) deep is dug with a base measuring 36in (915mm) square. Land drains of the earthenware pattern for preference (plastic is too slippery) are used to provide run-ins from the ground surface to four inlets at the bottom of the hole. The hole is covered with a lid (A) which has a separate door (a) and a central hole through this in which to insert a bait tethering pole. Steel traps are placed on the floor of the hole. If the set is pre-baited for a time, vermin will grow accustomed to entering. The traps should be in position but unsprung until it is obvious that the set is being visited regularly. At this stage they are tensioned and it is quite likely that three or four will each take a victim because the animals will have become accustomed to entering for food.

The bait can be a freshly killed bird, but it should have the skin torn open and be allowed to bleed in order to produce a tempting odour.

The trap can be selective in the animals that it will capture by

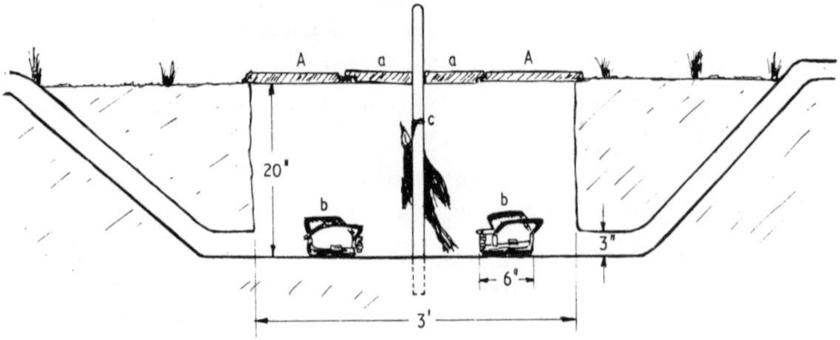

Fig 6 Instone trap

varying the size of the drains that are used. It also has an advantage in restricting its catch to those mammals that move underground. The same set could, of course, more humanely, use the newer types of spring traps approved for use in Britain.

If for any reason it is a problem to set traps underground or to bury them, then they can be used in a box-set. This is useful when children or domestic animals are about, or on estates where gamebirds are being conserved. The box serves as a tunnel with entrances which are too small for domestic animals to enter. Steel traps are placed inside with fresh bait between them, rather as in the Idstone trap set. In rural areas it would be useful to improvise tunnels by using flat stones or pieces of heavy tree bark, held together with a daub of wet clay and straw. Set in hedgerows or gaps in fences they can be effective because ground vermin see them as easy pathways through an apparent obstruction.

There is yet another set that can be used for animals attracted to burrows. It is known as the dirt-hole set, and requires a mound or bank into which a false underground run or burrow can be constructed. A hole some 3in (75mm) in diameter and 8in (200mm) deep is dug into the bank at an angle downwards from the surface. The purpose is to give an impression of a natural burrow. Bushes and sticks should be arranged as a lead-in to the hole and between these, some 12in (300mm) distant from the mouth of the hole, a double spring type of steel trap is buried in the conventional manner, with the springs set at 45 degrees to the jaws. A fetid bait, such as the corpse of a young rabbit, is thrown into the hole and to provide further attraction scent baits such as fox urine, or glandular scents, can be sprinkled in the nearby vegetation. Some trap suppliers also market various artificial lures, which can be effective if natural scent baits are not available. In the absence of a mound, a coop or cubby-set can be made from stones and twigs with a blind end and bait thrown in beyond the buried trap.

Using Steel Traps for Rats

Wherever there is livestock, especially poultry, and where there are food stores, especially granaries, rats are a problem. Poison, in the form of pastes, can be used, but there is a danger both to domestic animals and wild birds as well as the risk of contaminating stored food.

Other than using dogs, traps provide the best form of control. It is not surprising that many kinds of traps have been devised in order to combat the activities of these pests. It is worth considering that, more than all other pests, the rat is dangerous, not simply because it competes with man for his stores of food, but as a potential transmitter of diseases affecting humans. Mostly, the disease-causing organisms are transmitted by the fleas which infest the rats, but these can quite easily move on to human beings. Only by enforcing rigorous controls to prevent the black rats which often infest ships from getting ashore, have port health authorities been able to overcome the spread of rat-borne diseases such as bubonic plague—the Black Death of the Middle Ages. Also rat urine, especially when washed into water used by humans, can cause Weil's disease.

Steel traps have frequently been used for catching rats; in fact it is possible in places where steel traps can still legally be sold to buy so-called rat steel traps. Unfortunately these are small, usually with only 3in (75mm) jaws, and while they do what they are supposed to do—grip a rat by its leg—this is singularly inappropriate. Rats are rodents—gnawing animals—and they will quickly gnaw their way through their own limb in order to free themselves from a trap; in fact it has been known for other rats to assist in this operation in order to free one of their own kind. There are some traps designed for catching rats which have sharp-toothed jaws and these are quite useless because the

Fig 7 Rat rub marks on beam

released jaws can sever a limb directly. It does not seem to be so great a handicap for a rat to have a leg missing as it is for so many other four-legged creatures.

In practice it is best to use a trap with 5in (125mm) jaws because this will grip a rat around the head and body so that it has no chance of escape; indeed with traps of this size it is more likely that the sprung jaws will deal a lethal blow.

Rats are creatures of habit, usually making obvious and well-worn paths within and around buildings which they infest, so that traps can be sited on shelving and beams above the ground. In these places rats indicate their presence by means of the soiled rub-marks produced around upright beams and supports (see Figure 7). The traps are secured by their chains to an adjoining wall, but should be placed in line with the run and certainly at no greater angle than 45 degrees. If traps are placed at greater angles than this, when they are sprung by the rats the rising jaw nearest to the animals will be likely to lift them bodily and throw them clear, thus allowing them to escape.

Steel traps used in buildings in the manner described do not require to be baited, but neither they nor the surfaces on which they are placed should have any traces of human scent. Earlier warnings about rat traps carrying rat blood must be heeded.

The Terrier Signal Run trap (Figure 8) is a way of using a trap under cover and with a device to indicate when it has been sprung. It was invented by Mark Hovell and provides a means of catching rats while at the same time avoiding possible injury to domestic cats which might climb around the shelves and beams of a storeroom. The box provides entrances at both ends so that rats can enter from either direction when it is placed on a run, but once they are inside there are buttresses just in front of the trap jaws which force them to move over the pan, activate the trigger and so release the jaws. A cord attached to the jaw is slackened as the jaw rises and the lever fastened at the opposite end of the cord consequently dips, indicating a catch.

If the trap is used above ground level, say on a beam, it must be securely fastened with cord or wire, but the signal will be obvious at some distance below.

Looking After Steel Traps

Any mechanical device is only as efficient as its condition allows, so peak efficiency will be obtained only by careful attention to traps after they have been used.

New traps need to be boiled in water to which a small amount of caustic potash has been added, to remove an unnatural metallic odour and any surplus oil or grease. They are hung to dry until a thin layer of rust has coated them, then they are stained by simmering in a solution of logwood crystals or water containing the mashed hulls of walnuts. This will turn them black and again

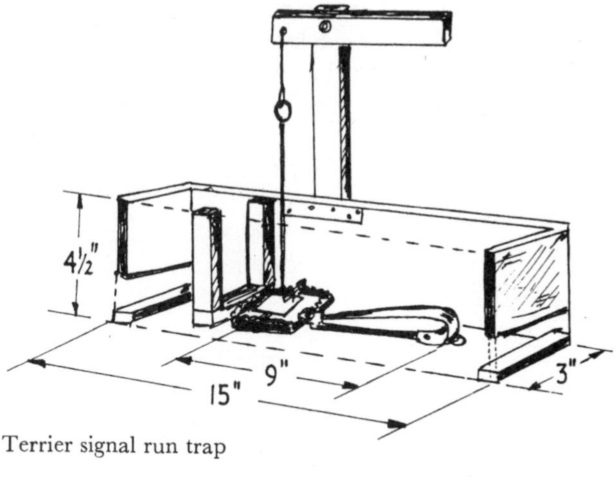

Fig 8 Terrier signal run trap

they are hung out to dry, care being taken to avoid handling them. Wooden tongs can be used to lift them from the staining bath and if hooks are hanging ready on a line, the traps can be suspended from their jaws. This treatment should be used after every trapping operation to remove traces of animal blood or human scent.

All the moving parts must have freedom of movement, so it is essential to inspect the rotation of the jaws in the eyes of the springs and the baseplate. Similarly, the dog or catch must move freely and also the shank of the tread pan.

Now that there is greater concern for health and safety, it would be imprudent to ignore the potential danger in using steel traps, not only in respect of animals which they have not been set to catch, but also for the trapper. It is necessary to appreciate that the bigger the trap the greater will be the potential force with which the jaws will close after the trap has been sprung and, therefore, the more serious the injury that could be inflicted upon a hand or foot accidentally in the pathway of snapping jaws.

In the past the trapping fraternity has enjoyed a reputation for fearlessness and toughness and while this is all very well, a preponderance of brawn is no substitute for a fair ration of brain when it comes to using steel traps. So the trapper who prides himself on being able, single-handed, to prime a double-spring 10in (250mm) trap might with benefit substitute some grey matter for muscle and get some assistance. Even more important, however capable a trapper may be, he should not cast scorn upon a pupil who cannot match his muscular feats. There are ways of priming steel traps that are safe and require only a minimum of effort.

Two sticks about 12in (300mm) long and 1in (25mm) thick are useful accessories. They should be flattened at one end for a distance of about 3in (75mm). A single person can manage a single spring trap, but double spring traps really need two people, because feet have to be used to depress the springs of large traps and one foot should always be on the ground. With the spring or springs depressed, after ensuring that the dog is thrown back, the flat end of one stick is used to turn a jaw outwards. It should be the jaw which is to be held down and the other stick should be used to throw the dog over it. The dog may have to be held down with the stick while the first one is used to raise the tread pan by passing the stick under the free jaw. The notch on the pan must be caught by the dog over the fixed jaw. The stick is pushed *under* the free jaw to avoid having it caught, should the jaws accidentally snap shut. The free jaw is finally lowered until it is level with the fixed one.

When a primed trap has to be carried, even for a short distance, it should be held by the lower end of the spring and hands should never be moved into the area bounded by the jaws. Gloves should be worn in order to avoid tainting the traps with human scent. An industrial pattern will also offer some protection in case of an accident. Different gloves should be used for carrying fresh and used traps.

Steel traps are sized on the basis of the length of an individual jaw, but in a 6in (150mm) trap, the space bounded by the jaws when they are spread open will be 6in (150mm) square. Although traps as small as $1\frac{1}{2}$in (38mm) are known, the usual range is from about 3in (75mm) up to 16in (400mm), the smallest size being for animals like chipmunks and the largest for bears. Manufacturers often use numbers to identify their trap sizes, but these are unreliable because there is no universal system, so that a number 6 of one manufacturer might be a 5in (125mm) rabbit trap, while a number 6 of another maker could be a 16in (400mm) bear trap.

Apart from the traps, a trapper needs some accessories, the chief of which is a suitable spade. Trappers' spades can be purchased, but the short-handled lightweight type with a pointed blade, as used by army commandos, is ideal and it is sometimes possible to get hold of these from government surplus supply stores. The sharp pointed blade is most useful if traps have to be buried in hard ground.

Pegs and staples, either wooden or steel, are needed for anchoring small traps, but clogs have to be made when catching larger animals. For catching a bear or a big cat it would be preferable to anchor the trap to a felled tree trunk.

Soil which is sprinkled over a buried trap should be sieved to remove any gravel, otherwise there is a risk that this would obstruct the jaws when the trap is sprung.

Traps should have a swivel joint to which an anchoring chain is attached, but this is not always a standard feature, although a blacksmith would find no difficulty in adding one. Suitable chains are also necessary, the lengths varying according to the distances likely to separate traps and clogs.

Trapping Skill

The measure of expertise in using steel traps can be measured in various ways. Where long lines of traps are put out a simple measure would be the catch-to-trap ratio which, for a given space of time, is derived from the proportion of animals caught to the number of traps laid. On a more selective basis, the quantity of the type of animal for which the traps have been set compared with the total number caught, is a stern test of trapping skill. While admitting that steel traps are largely and intrinsically non-selective, a high degree of selectivity can be introduced by relating the setting technique to the known habits of the animals concerned.

Baits

Apart from the fineness with which traps are primed, the places chosen as sites and the ways in which they are concealed, the one other essential piece of trapping lore which can increase the catch is a knowledge of using baits.

There are no hard and fast rules about using baits and the decision about which to use will depend upon the kind of trap and set being employed, the animal to be attracted and the weather conditions at the times.

Animals vary in their responses to the environments. Some have keen sight and use this to locate a prey or detect an enemy, while others depend upon their hearing. A sense of smell, either to detect food or the scent of a member of the opposite sex, can be very important. There are also some greedy animals that at the sight and smell of food will abandon most if not all of their normal caution.

For animals with co-dominant senses, such as a cats which have acute vision, especially in poor light, as well as good hearing, it is often possible to distract one of these faculties. While cats can manipulate their ears freely to concentrate upon the source of a sound, they will often turn their head away from the direction of the sound when something strange falls into their line of vision. With animals having good vision, it is more often than not a movement which attracts their attention, rather than a particular shape.

Live animals have been used as bait, rabbits for foxes, and puppies for wolves, but this is a practice which is frowned upon for humanitarian reasons, because although they attract attention when they move or utter a cry, there are alternative baits that can be used.

Most baits have some form of scent-producing property and this can be very useful, but it depends upon the ability of substances to produce vapours which will travel through the atmosphere to excite the nasal sense organs of animals. The weather conditions must therefore favour evaporation of scent vapours, and whereas some warmth is beneficial, too much will dry out the bait and make it useless. It follows that if trapping has to be undertaken in hot weather, the traps and the bait must be placed in the shade in order to preserve the bait; a further advantage will be that in these conditions the shade is also likely to attract the animals almost as much as the bait will.

Some scents seem to be generally appealing to animals. Among those which seem to have no apparent basis for their appeal are caraway, sweet oil, oil of anise and oil of rhodium. The cat family, including wild and domestic species, civet cats, servals, lynx, jaguars, leopards, cheetahs, lions and tigers, are all attracted by the extract of the plant *Nepeta*, usually known as catnip. Similarly, the dog family, including domestic dogs, foxes, coyotes, jackals and wolves respond to valerian, which is a product of the plants of the *Valeriana* group. Oil of anise, which comes from species of the plant *Pimpinella*, while having a widespread attractiveness as a bait, has a particular appeal to bears of all kinds.

The natural products of the bodies of animals, especially their excretions and secretions, can often be used as baits for species of their own kind. Included here are the droppings, or faeces, urine and extracts from scent glands of the kinds possessed by foxes, polecats and beavers. Many animals use both urine and faeces to mark their territorial boundaries. The dog family and the mustelids are noted for this activity and others of their kind can be induced to visit marked traps since they will wish to re-mark these spots with their own excreta.

Live animals have also been used as a sexual bait, for example a female in season, but this should be considered in the same manner as other instances of using live bait. There are usually alternatives which avoid suffering on the part of a decoy animal.

Finally among the natural scent baits are the secretions of scent glands found in animals such as beavers, skunks, polecats and mongooses. Beavers have scent glands which are to be found on either side of the anal opening; these are the castors. They can easily be dissected from a dead beaver as long as care is taken not, instead, to remove some other glands which are found lower down. The castors can be dried and then ground to powder, which is mixed with glycerin and in this form is used as a lure on a trap or in an area surrounding a trap. The scent glands of other animals can be treated and used in the same way.

Of all the baits which have been used, by far the largest number have been food baits. The kind of food used will be related to the diets of the animals being trapped. Animals which are mainly graniferous (seed eaters) can be attracted by soaked grains of cereals, especially maize, wheat or barley. One recipe for a rat bait includes 1lb (454g) flour, 1lb (454g) breadcrumbs, 3oz (85g) grated cheese and 3oz (85g) treacle or molasses. Another uses 1lb (454g) oatmeal, 3 drops each of caraway and anise oils, 4 drops of oil of rhodium and some powdered musk, but opinion has it that the battery of volatile oils does more in covering up human scent than in attracting rats.

Some mammals are frugivorous (fruit eating), and a number that are not nevertheless seem partial to fruit if it is used as a bait. Many fruits, particularly citrus and bananas, have strongly attracting scents, but even apples can prove very effective baits and have been used successfully for capturing squirrels, muskrats and opossums.

It is quite obvious that the best bait for a carnivore will be meat and for most of them it must be fresh, as there is little attraction from meat when it has dried up. Joints can be hung up for large mammals, but often a paunched carcass is better, especially in warm climates, as it will dry out less quickly. There are some animals—carrion feeders—which are attracted by fetid meat. Included here are some members of the dog family, such as foxes and jackals, which will eat either freshly killed meat or carrion. Fetid bait can be made from chopped raw fish that is kept for a month in a tin with a perforated lid to allow the gases to escape.

If baits are difficult to produce or acquire from ready-to-hand sources, it is often possible to purchase them from trap suppliers. These baits are proprietary preparations and tend to be specifics for groups such as rabbits, foxes, muskrats, skunks, rodents, squirrels and chipmunks and are usually packed as pastes in tins designed to serve 25, 50 or 100 sets. In the United States Hawbaker's baits are marketed by the Allcock Manufacturing Co.

One or two tips to be observed when using baits should prove useful. Pre-baiting has already been mentioned and while it obviously slows down the trapping programme, it can often repay the waiting time in terms of the ultimate size of the catch. Baits are also used to lead-in animals towards a trap, especially if using a set which induces the lead-in by having sticks or bushes flanking the approach to the buried trap.

It is not usual to attach baits to a leg-hold trap and so if baits are needed near to a trap they are either hung above from a pole, or placed beyond the trap, as in the cubby-hole or dirt-hole sets.

As a last word about baits in this section it would seem that trappers stick to certain proven recipes, that is those which seem to work for them; but there is no guarantee that a bait will be universally successful, probably because it is not so much what is used, but rather how it is used that counts. Anyone new to trapping would be well advised to try various baits from the lists of those recommended and, by experimenting with them in different sets, hope to come up with a selection that works.

Humane Spring Traps

Within this category is a whole range of comparatively recently produced traps. They are mostly the products of an endeavour to meet with objections to the use of leg-hold and similar inhumane forms of traps. They are also in response to legislation in many countries which is out-lawing the steel leg-hold trap. The purposes of the new traps are to kill animals as humanely and as quickly as possible, with the additional wish to make trapping much more selective and so avoid unintentional killing.

Spring traps which have at least a 90 per cent killing success are by no means new. The long-established break-back traps, which have been used for controlling rats and mice, fall into this category.

Among the humane spring traps developed in Britain there is none that will take an animal larger than a rabbit, but, with the exception of foxes which are not protected, the main vermin worrying gamekeepers, who are the principal trap users, are weasels, stoats, rats and grey squirrels, and all of these can be taken with the traps available.

The range of spring traps developed in Britain as a result of the activities of the Humane Traps Advisory Committee set up in 1954 by the Minister for Agriculture, Fisheries and Food and the Department of Agriculture and Fisheries for Scotland, were largely based upon designs which included a pair of vertically striking arms arranged to apply a lethal blow to an animal's head or neck and also to grip it. From 1954 onwards experimental

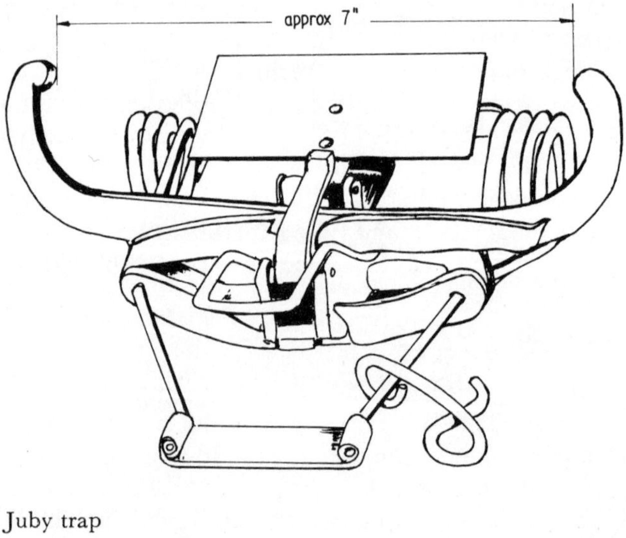

Fig 9 Juby trap

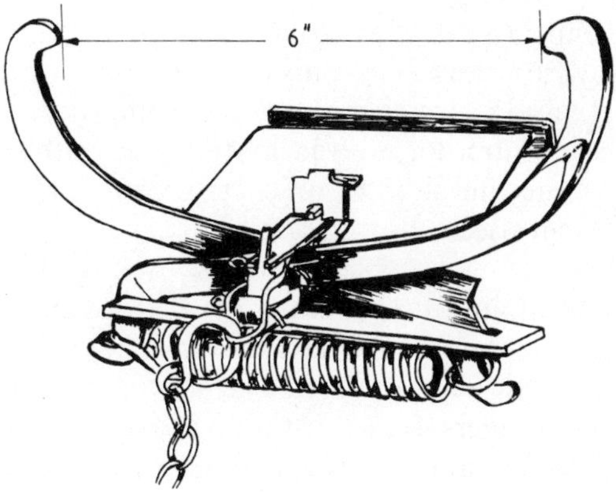

Fig 10 Imbra trap

work was undertaken by the National Institute of Agricultural Engineering and resulting from this and the work of individuals it was possible to introduce government approval for a Spring Traps Approval Order in 1957. This nominated traps given the seal of approval because they functioned in the way outlined above. The traps specifically detailed in the Order and in subsequent Amending Orders now include Fenn Vermin Traps Marks 1 to 4, the Sawyer, Juby, Lloyd, Imbra Marks 1 and 2 and the Fuller.

The Approval Orders and subsequent amendments not only specified traps but also described the manner in which they could be used and the animals for which they could be set.

Juby and Imbra traps are mainly useful for controlling rabbits and squirrels (see Figures 9 and 10), but only the Juby is still manufactured, although Imbra traps might be found from time to time in sales of second-hand farm and estate equipment. They can be used only in rabbit holes for taking rabbits, but if used for grey squirrels, stoats, weasels, rats and other small vermin, they must be used in specially constructed tunnels.

Of the remaining traps, only the Fenn Mark 4 and the Lloyd are still manufactured. They are used for small ground vermin including weasels, stoats and grey squirrels, and again they must be set inside naturally occurring or artificially constructed tunnels. Rats and mice can be taken with these traps and it is permissible for this purpose to set them in runs in the open. While officially permissible, great care should be observed in ensuring that, as far as is possible, other animals such as domestic cats or small dogs are not injured by traps set in the open.

Although it has been stressed that leg-hold traps cannot be used in Britain as pole traps, it should be quite clear that the newer humane spring traps must not be used in this way either. There have been instances where Fenn traps have been used illegally as pole traps and when the users have been discovered and prosecuted they have been severely fined. This is mainly as a result of the activities of inspectors of the RSPB. Although designated as humane, the new spring traps can cause a considerable amount of suffering when used as pole traps or in any other unauthorized fashion.

The Fenn Trap

This is probably the most popular of the British humane spring traps. It has been used in a number of experimental field trials

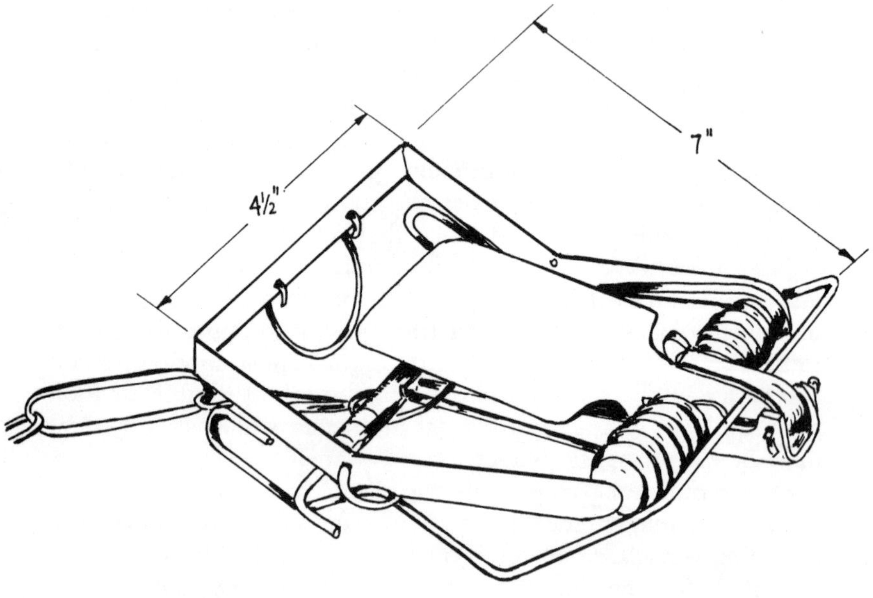

Fig 11 Fenn Mark IV trap

designed to estimate its efficiency and it is apparent that not only will lines of these traps provide adequate protection for young gamebirds on keepered estates from the attacks of ground vermin, but in 90 per cent of captures they achieve a fast and painless kill. Where this is not so, it is usually because they have not been set sufficiently finely.

Many gamekeepers nurtured on gin traps were reluctant to adopt the new traps, but those who have persevered now find them quite satisfactory. This is not to suggest that the Fenn Mark 4 is the ultimate in traps and it is likely that better instruments will be available in the future.

Newly purchased Fenn traps should, like steel traps, be weathered or buried in earth for a time in order to remove the factory and metallic smells which some animals might find repugnant.

Before being used for the first time the catch should be filed back, because if set without this refinement most of the traps would set coarse and many animals, especially the small ones, would be too light in weight to spring a trap. The plate and the jaws should be level when the trap is set; if they are not, the plate neck should be turned down a small amount to achieve this. It is also likely that the wire loop for attaching the chain to the trap will need to be flattened, otherwise the trap will rock up and down when it is set.

The traps must be set in tunnels and a variety of styles can be used. Old traditional materials, such as stone, rocks, bricks, turf or wood are reasonable in their way, but if six dozen traps are to be set around a shoot it would involve considerable carting and time-consuming building to get them all in place. Better by far are ready-made drainage pipes and there is a choice of clay or pitch fibre, preferably 6in (150mm) diameter. Clay will be heavy to carry about and liable to break more easily; furthermore, clay pipes only come in 12in (300mm) lengths, but 18in (450mm) is much the more preferable size. It is best therefore to choose 18in lengths of pitch fibre pipe. They should have a vertical oval hole 2 by 1in (50 by 25mm) drilled in the tube at a distance of 6in (150mm) from one end. This is to take the catch when the trap is set inside.

The siting of the tunnels will depend upon the animals for

which the traps are being set. Most ground vermin have regular runs and favourite tunnel sites include gaps in hedges, gateways, through piles of fallen timber in woods and gaps in stone walls. The dried-up bottom of a drainage ditch can be used on a temporary basis, but would be no use as a permanent tunnel site because of the risk of filling with water.

When a site has been chosen a groove is cut into the ground with a spade, allowing the tube to sink for one-third of its height into the ground. Three sods of grass are cut, each about 2ft (600mm) long, 8in (200mm) wide and as thick as possible. One is placed on either side of the fibre tube and the third goes on the top as a keystone. They are pushed together and trimmed to leave a grassy overhanging fringe at each end. Not only will this look immediately natural, but the thickness of the sods will allow continued growth and an increasingly natural appearance as time goes on. A bucketful of fine sieved earth or leaf-mould is prepared and pushed through the mouth of the liner tube to fill it up to the level of the ground outside, thus providing a permanent bed in which the trap can be repeatedly set.

The trap should have a wooden or metal peg about 8in (200mm) long attached to the chain. The peg is driven into the ground and out of sight of the mouth of the tunnel; this will be easier if the peg is a metal one. The trap is set as finely as possible with the catch in place, then it is pushed into the tunnel as far as the chain will allow and finally placed in a previously formed hollow in the sieved-leaf-litter floor with the catch fitted into the hole made earlier in the tunnel tube. The position of the trap, the floor of the tunnel and the ground outside should all be uniformly level and this can be judged only by lying prone. Some fine leaf mould is sprinkled over the trap to mask its outline and the safety catch is removed with a piece of wire. A run-in can be cut in front of the trap to guide animals towards it. No further camouflage is really necessary.

When a Fenn is sprung the jaws move in an arc which follows the circumference of the 6in (150mm) diameter tube, leaving about $\frac{1}{4}$in (6mm) to spare if the tunnel has been constructed exactly in the manner described.

The distribution of the traps will depend upon the topography of the estate and this needs careful advance planning. Also, the accessibility for inspection by a keeper has to be taken into account, remembering that legislation and humanitarian considerations require the inspection of each set trap at least once every twenty-four hours. Regular inspection can ensure that sprung traps are speedily reset, because if left sprung they will catch nothing further.

These rather extended instructions can be followed with only minor variations when using the Sawyer and Lloyd traps. A Sawyer trap (see Figure 12), now unavailable except secondhand, is fundamentally like the Fenn; the main difference is that the release mechanism is at the spring end in a Fenn and at the opposite end in a Sawyer. The Lloyd trap is much more like a leg-hold trap when viewed superficially because, instead of using coiled springs working equally on each jaw, it has a baseplate from which a wire spring projects towards the jaws. As seen in the illustration on page 67 this has a loop at the jaw end which surrounds the pivoted bases of the jaws. One jaw is fixed and has a bar running across it over which the catch is placed when the trap is set. Beyond the bar, the plain wire jaw is bent at an

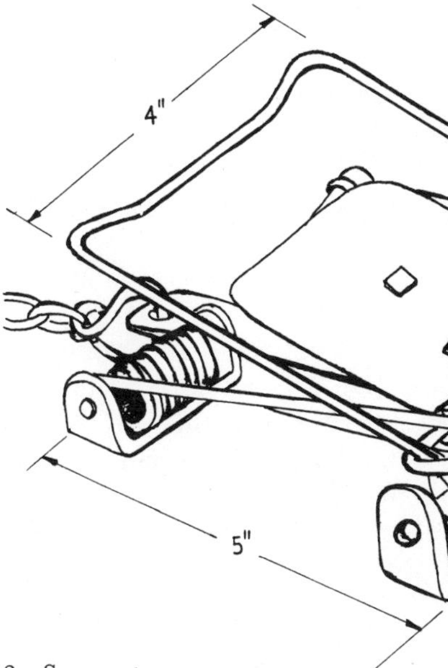

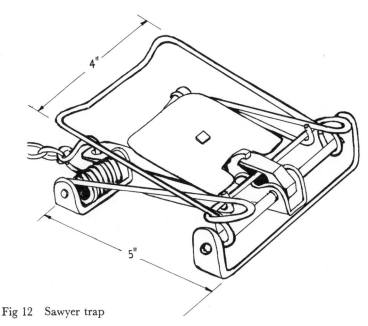

Fig 12 Sawyer trap

angle of 90 degrees when set and so is vertical. The free jaw is similarly bent, although at a slightly smaller angle. Herein lies the difference from a leg-hold trap, which when set has its jaws flat on the ground. When a Lloyd trap is sprung the animal's body is enveloped by the jaws and generally it is killed.

The Juby trap is now the main one readily available for catching rabbits in Britain; superficially it is like the Imbra trap which it has largely replaced. It is intended to be used only inside a rabbit hole, but if used for grey squirrels and small vermin such as stoats and weasels it must be set inside a tunnel. Tunnels constructed for Fenn traps would be too small for the Juby, which is quite large. The usual method of siting these big traps is to employ a two-piece tunnel, as seen in the illustration on page 68, which shows a squirrel taken in an Imbra trap set in such a tunnel.

The Juby trap in the set position is shown in Figure 9 on page 36. The advantage of a Juby over a gin or steel trap which it has replaced for taking rabbits, is the presence of a safety catch. This is a protection for the trapper, because steel traps are exceedingly dangerous when being carried around in a set position. A Juby has two coil springs which are joined by bows, one of which links the adjacent ends of the springs and the other the extreme ends. The bow from the extreme ends provides axle pivots on which the bases of the two arms or jaws can rotate. The arms can only be opened fully if the bow joining the adjacent ends of the springs is depressed, then the catch is placed over the lowered arms and engaged on the pan trigger.

When a Juby trap is used for catching rabbits it must be set inside a hole which has an overhang. A depression is dug in the floor of the hole, some distance in from the mouth, so that when the trap is in place and set, the pan is just below ground level; it is then covered with sifted earth or leaf mould so that the arms cannot be seen. It must be placed so that the emerging rabbit will put its fore-paws on the pan, which means that the arms will be at the entrance-facing end of the trap. The trap action when sprung ensures that the rabbit is taken about its neck and killed outright, but daily inspection of traps is required by law to account for the very few instances when rabbits are not killed immediately.

Conibear Trap

In North America there is one trap which has been developed to provide for humane killing of pests and fur bearers. This is the trap developed by Frank Conibear, a British Columbian trapper who had the support of the Canadian Association for Humane Trapping, the Vancouver SPCA, the British Columbian SPCA, and the Association for the Protection of Furbearing Animals. It was first marketed in 1958, since when a variety of models has appeared to deal with mammals of different sizes. Apart from its humane action, it has the advantage of being adaptable to a variety of sets, including trail sets, under-water sets and under-ice sets (see Figure 13).

The Conibear 120 has a 4½in (108mm) square jaw spread and is intended primarily for catching muskrats, although it can be used in Britain for grey squirrels when used in a tunnel. The 110 can be used for weasels, stoats and squirrels, but although suggested for mink, it is probably not sufficiently powerful to kill these animals humanely and quickly because of their robust neck muscles.

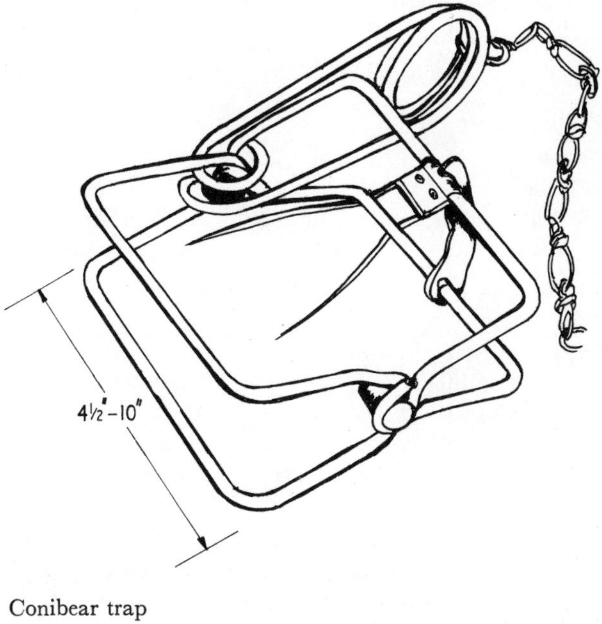

Fig 13 Conibear trap

A number 220 Conibear has not proved to be either quick enough or powerful enough in action and is not recommended. The giant of the series with 10in (250mm) square jaw spread is the 330. This was developed especially for taking beavers and has proved itself admirable for the purpose, especially in a drowning set. Otters and wolves can be taken when it is used in a head set and it can also be successful with foxes, coyotes, lynx, wolverines, martens, fishers, racoons and badgers. When altered to provide a jaw spread of 9 by 8in (230 by 200mm) it has proved valuable in Britain for trapping coypus.

The Conibear trap has two scissor-hinged and four-sided jaws made of metallic rod. A forked trigger is fastened to the side of one jaw, while the opposite side of the other is the dog, or catch. At an angle to the coil springs are two arms which end in loops to encircle the two jaws. The jaws can be rotated to allow the dog to engage a slot on the hinge of the trigger when the arms of the spring are compressed together. If considered desirable, the trigger can be baited and when it is released the whole mechanism is reversed to catch an animal about its neck or middle which usually kills it. The trap has some of the characteristics of a jump trap, because when an animal is caught the trap springs up dealing a lethal blow to the head. There can be up to three striking surfaces.

Although the use of the trap is unrestricted in Canada, it has been prohibited in some densely populated parts of the United States because of its potential danger to children and domestic animals when set on land. The 330 has been shown to kill a beaver in a water set within three to four seconds by breaking its neck.

Mole Traps

There are two kinds of mole traps approved as humane in Britain and both of these are spring operated.

The Duffus trap, seen in the illustration on page 101, is an example of a half-round barrel trap, so called because of the half-cylindrical cover, compared with a full barrel-shaped cylinder found in earlier and now obsolete mole traps. From the illustration it will be clear that there are two wire nooses, one of which is shown set and the other sprung. The nooses can be pressed through slots in the metal cover and each is under the separate control of a double coil spring. Each spring also has its own trigger, so that when the trap is placed in an underground mole run it is possible for a mole to be caught regardless of the direction from which it approaches the trap; in fact, unless the vibration of one noose being sprung also releases the second, it is possible for two moles to be caught in the same trap.

The trap is placed in one of the runs that moles make just below the surface of the ground. The run is carefully opened from the surface so that the holes at either end of the opening are not blocked. The trap is lowered into the run, having been set as finely as possible. Finely sifted soil or leaf mould is sprinkled over the trap and when the trap has been sprung this will be obvious from the arms holding the nooses, which will now have penetrated through the surface.

When deciding where to place mole traps, due regard must be paid to any signs of mole activity. The obvious feature is the mole hill which results from the soil pushed up vertical shafts from the horizontal runs. Freshly produced mounds will indicate recent burrowing and suggest places to put traps. This can be assisted by

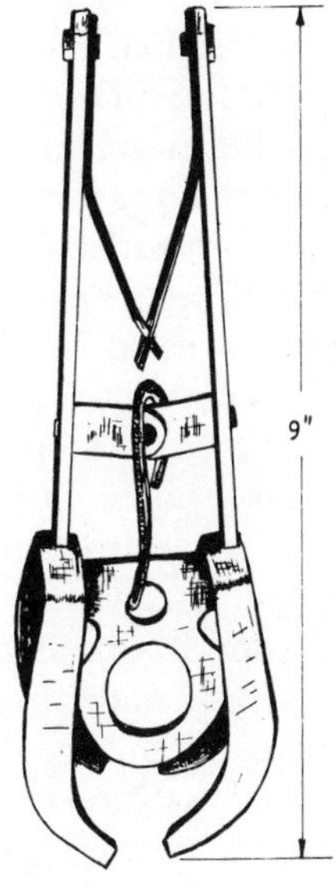

Fig 14 Scissor-type mole trap

pushing thin sticks into the ground between the mounds to discover where there is little resistance and therefore the likelihood of a burrow. Sometimes when the runs are close to the ground surface, the vibration of the ground from a burrowing mole can be noticeable.

The second most popular mole trap is the tongs or scissor type seen in Figure 14. The drawing shows a trap set in a position as if the mole run were running through the page. There are two steel jaws which have metal bars above and these are linked by a central hinge which provides the scissors action. Tension comes from leaf springs riveted to the tops of the bars and pressing against each other lower down. A hook over the hinge has a metal tongue which serves the double purpose of holding the jaws apart and acting as a trigger.

A hole big enough for the jaws is cut into a mole tunnel just below the ground surface. The trap is set and placed with the tongue facing the direction of the tunnel in such a manner that a mole running along the tunnel will strike the tongue, dislodge it and thereby release the jaws and the spring tension. The result is that the mole will be struck around its middle by the sprung jaws and quickly killed. When the trap is placed in the tunnel the usual advice is to cover it over with sifted soil or leaf-mould to ground level, leaving the bars protruding. The change in the appearance of these when a trap is sprung is an indication that inspection is necessary. Some mole trappers have found it advantageous not to seal the hole containing the trap with soil. The explanation is that moles do not like draughts in their burrows and will come along the tunnel to close the gap, but in doing this they blunder into the trap. In the United States under the Victor trade mark it is still possible to buy a guillotine type of trap. Two prongs hold it in the ground above a run and a powerful vertical spring releases a six-pointed plunger. It takes a fair amount of effort to set the trap because the plate holding the six pointed spikes has to be pushed back against the spring tension in order to engage a notch in the hinged metal bar at the top of the frame. The bar, in turn, is secured by another hinged catch on one side which also serves as a trigger. When a mole pushes through its run and strikes the trigger, the spring tension is released and the spikes plunge downwards to kill it.

Gopher Trap

In the United States the pocket gopher is a pest equivalent to moles in Britain. Like moles, gophers construct extensive underground networks of runs and similarly they push soil above the surface to produce mounds. The runs can vary in depth from 1ft (300mm) to just below the surface. Apart from damaging lawns, this rodent also attacks garden bulbs and root vegetables, at night as well as during the day. So numerous and prolific are they that eradication seems to be well nigh impossible. None the less, gardeners try to control them and trapping is often the safest and most efficient method.

The traps, one of which is seen in Figure 15, are used in pairs within a cone-shaped hole dug where a hill has been thrown up. They are placed one either side of the hole, facing in opposite directions, with their claw-like jaws away from the holes. The traps are anchored to pegs outside the burrows. The burrows must be well cleaned out to prevent the traps from being fouled and also to avoid warning the gopher that its run has suffered interference. The gophers are sensitive to light, so the hole is covered over with a sod of turf, previously moistened to prevent soil from crumbling into the hole and blocking the trap mechanism. When an animal comes along its burrow it will push against the upright plate of the trap and so release the trigger, held in a hole pierced in the lower part of the plate. The released trigger no longer holds down the jaws and they spring up to close around the body of the gopher.

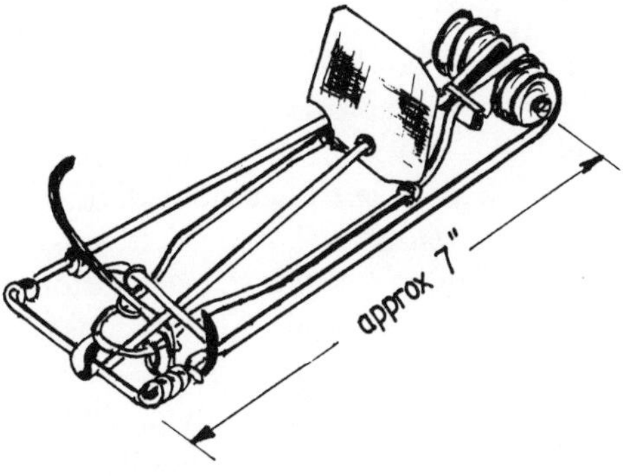

Fig 15 Pocket gopher trap

Mouse Traps

Of all the mammal pests with which man has had to contend throughout history, mice figure almost universally, while methods for controlling them have abounded in literature from times predating the dawn of the printing press.

House mice compete with man for his stores of food and they invade the cellars and the roof spaces of his homes. Field mice frequently cause extensive damage to cultivated crops and they are an especial nuisance when they attack plantations of seedling trees. For these various reasons and because of their prolific

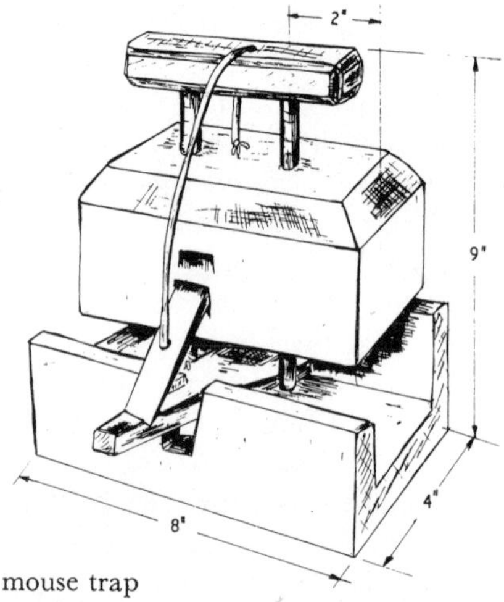

Fig 16 Deadfall mouse trap

breeding rate, they have made enemies of householders, storekeepers, farmers, foresters and shopkeepers.

There must have been hundreds of different kinds of mouse traps invented over the course of man's existence on earth; some of these have been killers, like the comparatively recent and still popular break-back types, some are live traps, normally based upon a box or cage, and a few have been automatic repeating models designed to deal with mouse infestations of a large scale.

Some quite effective mouse traps can be home-made by any handyman able to construct things out of timber. The model shown in Figure 16 is of a deadfall type and while it is a little bulky it is still perfectly portable. The tray measures approxi-

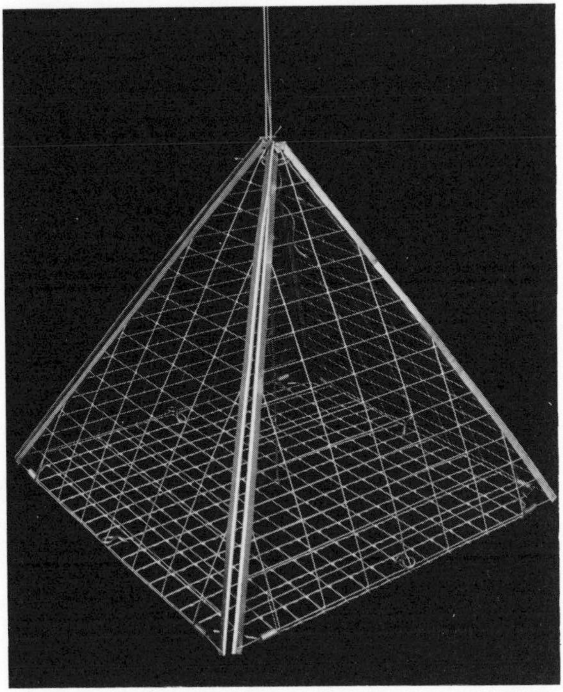

Star crab trap ready for hauling

A portable fish trap

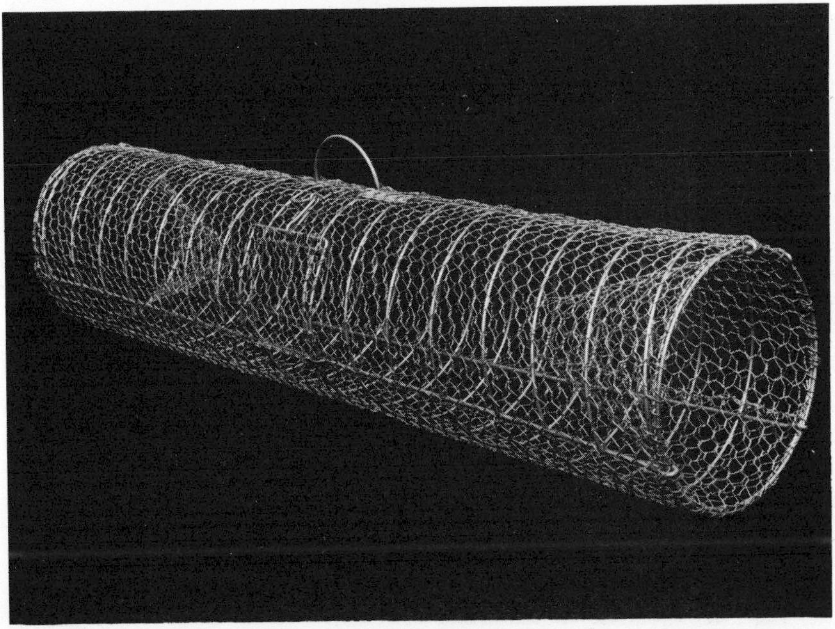

Putchers on the River Severn

A sparrow trap

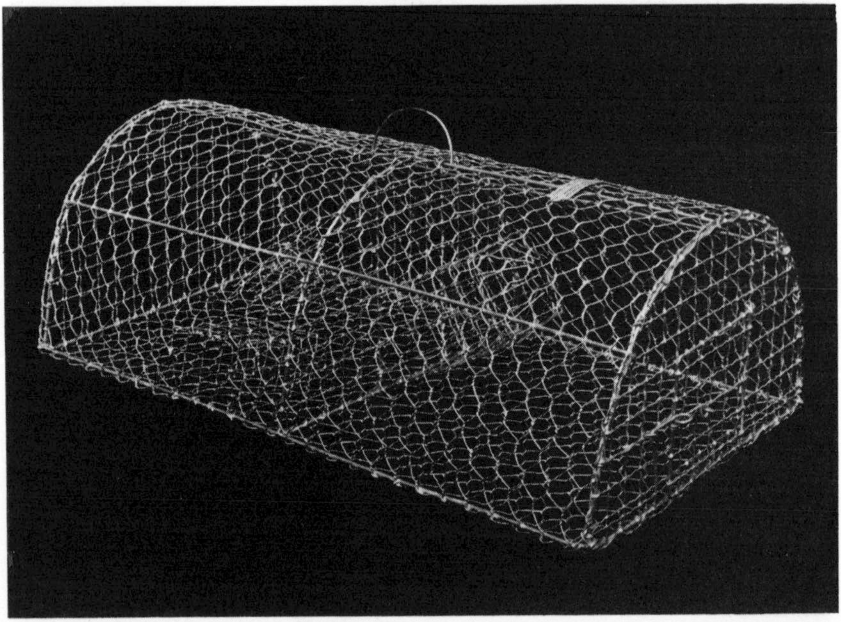

mately 8 by 4in (200 by 100mm) and from its base there are two upright dowel rods extending vertically, 2in (50mm) from each end, to a height of about 9in (230mm). Their tops are joined by a wooden bar drilled to receive them. A wooden block serving as the deadfall weight is sized to fit inside the tray and is drilled in appropriate positions to slide up and down on the dowels. There is a string cord fastened through the mid-point of the bar connecting the tops of the dowels. One end is fastened to the mid-point of the block and the other to the trigger. One end of this trigger is notched into a groove carved in the side of the weight and the other similarly into the paddle. The paddle has a narrow end which fits through a slot cut into the side of the tray and the broader end pivots at the base of the other side. Bait is placed on the paddle, with some more leading into the tray. When a mouse steps on the paddle, provided that this is set sufficiently finely, it will dislodge the trigger and the weight will drop on to the mouse.

The trap shown in Figure 17 is another deadfall type which can be made by a handyman, but it is an improvement on the previous one as the tray is replaced by a box and this is able to function as a tunnel. The box is built from ½in (12mm) timber to dimensions of 1ft (300mm) in length, 4in (100mm) width and a

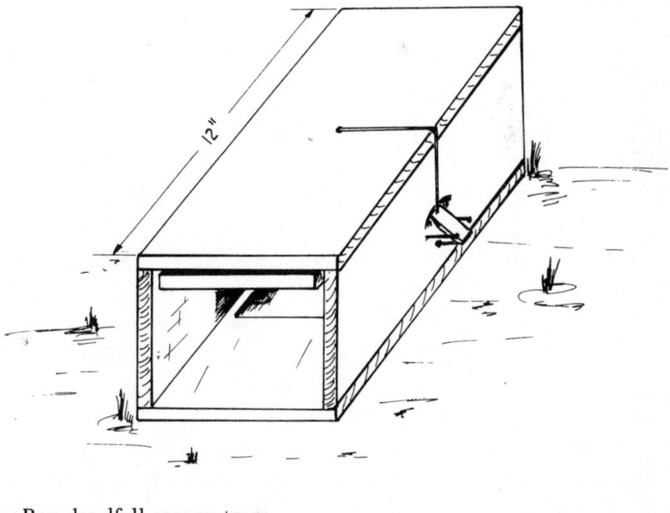

Fig 17 Box deadfall mouse trap

height of 6in (150mm). It is open-ended to function as a tunnel and the deadfall weight is a 1in (25mm) thick block, just less than the length and width of the inside of the box so that the sides function as guides when it drops. The centre of the floor of the box has a 3in (75mm) square hole cut into it and inside this is a tin-plate treadle platform having wire pivots soldered to its under surface. The pivot on one side goes into the wooden floor, while the other goes through the floor to emerge on the side of the box. A trigger is attached to the protruding wire and caught in a notch higher up on the side of the box. From the trigger a waxed cord passes upwards and then down through a hole in the top of the box to fasten to the block inside.

The platform is baited and the trap set in a run used by mice. When a mouse treads on the platform the trigger is released and the block descends. As a tunnel trap it can be used for field mice, but it should be camouflaged with twigs and grass, making sure that the trigger action is not in any way fouled.

Among break-back mouse traps there are many different patterns, some of which are made from combinations of wire and wood, whereas some are all metal. Apart from the materials used in their construction the main variations are in the mechanism of the trigger release, the type of spring employed and the incorporation of an automatic setting device to prevent damage to the trapper's fingers from a premature release of the spring. There are also a range of bait-holding structures which include a pair of wire prongs on the trigger, and a hook projecting from a tin-plate trigger.

One example of a break-back trap, the Victor made in the United States, has proved very popular and efficient in terms of the catch-to-trap ratio possible when it is used in large numbers. This seems to be the result of a double-catch release mechanism which allows for setting both coarsely and finely and also gives a two-way action. The last feature is made possible by having a small nick in the side of the tin-plate trigger. Thus if a mouse pulls at the bait trigger from in front it will release the catch and, similarly, if it knocks the trigger from the side. Those traps which have a one-way catch release and which are set coarsely, often have all the bait removed without the catch being released.

The automatic setting trap is an all-metal type sold in Britain under the brand name Selfset. These are galvanized steel traps and they incorporate a lever which brings back a wire jaw and allows a catch to engage a trigger when it is depressed. The apparent advantage of this is to avoid having fingers injured in the event of the catch slipping, something not uncommon with break-back traps. On the other hand, if the trap is to be effective the setting should be fine. Unfortunately, by the same token, if the automatic mechanism is to work it can only do so when the trap is set fairly coarsely. It seems to work with the rat-trap version because the heavier animal releases the catch, but on the mouse trap, which is not a great deal smaller than the rat trap, the coarse setting is sometimes too much for a mouse to dislodge. It can be made finer by manipulating the catch and trigger, but then it is difficult to set automatically because the mechanism keeps slipping. The advertised advantage of this trap is that it can be set in the dark—useful in unlit cellars or roof spaces.

It has been suggested that some of the spring traps mentioned in the previous sections could be used for mice, particularly the Fenn Mark 4, the Lloyd and also the Conibear 110. These are quite powerfully sprung traps and while it is possible that some field mice or voles might be caught, it is unlikely, even when finely set, that they would catch smaller mice.

Baits are essential with all the traps mentioned so far, because the success of the traps depends upon a mouse pulling at the bait on the trigger hook. There are all kinds of baits to attract mice, but the field is narrowed when it has to be something to attach to a hook. It also has to remain on the hook when the mouse starts to nibble at it. Alternatively, if a deadfall trap is to be used, the bait must be compressible, otherwise when the weight drops it will not catch a mouse if it is obstructed by the bait. Surprisingly, mice can push their way through exceedingly narrow gaps and as little as ½in (13mm) would be enough to allow a fully grown house mouse to escape.

For attaching to the bait hooks on break-back traps, the following are recommended: beef suet, pieces of dried fruit such as apple rings or apricots and soaked grains of maize, wheat or barley threaded on to cotton with a needle and tied.

Where bait has to be spread or sprinkled as a lead-in to a trap, or used inside a deadfall trap, it can include crushed oats or oatmeal, flour, biscuit crumbs, small seeds as used for cage birds, peanut butter and dripping.

Some care should be taken in siting mouse traps. Mice usually leave droppings regularly in places where they are moving about, particularly where they have been undisturbed, and traps can be put into such an area. They can be set on the floor but care must be taken that they cannot injure domestic animals. Although a mouse trap may not directly cause serious injury to a small cat or dog, the animal would suffer shock and might injure itself trying to remove the trap.

Break-back traps are best positioned above the ground as mice find little difficulty in climbing up on to the shelves and ledges, and in this way domestic animals and children will be protected. There is a further advantage in that traps set high up will suffer less chance of being sprung accidentally from vibrations of people walking over the floor. When setting a trap on a shelf this should be sufficiently wide to prevent the trap being dislodged over the edge before it has caught its victim.

If mouse traps are being used in fields or woods to catch field mice, they should be placed in runs which can easily be seen under bushes, in hedgerows and in the bottom of long grass. They should not be put down in places over which people will walk or animals graze. If a large number of traps are being put out and concealed in grass and undergrowth, unless the trapper has a phenomenal memory, there should be some kind of guide to their distribution. A numbered list in a field notebook which gives the sequence of the traps in the line and a short description of each site can help. Otherwise, the places where traps have been deposited can be indicated using the gipsy lore of twisting vegetation into a knot, leaving a visible broken twig hanging down and marking the bark of a tree.

Automatic Mouse Traps

It is seldom that mice, especially house mice, come in ones and twos. They can easily reach plague proportions—in fact this has frequently occurred where there has been a mass attack on rats so leaving a vacant niche in which mice quickly fit.

In these circumstances, if trapping is part of the campaign, the use of multicatch and automatic traps can be successful. These are usually boxes of wood or metal and they incorporate some mechanism which allows mice to enter, but prevents them from leaving.

A sophisticated example is the Ketch-All marketed by Havahart in the United States. This is constructed from galvanized steel and consists of a box with a sliding lid. Inside there are three compartments: at one end are the works which provide the clockwork drive for the three-vaned paddle in the central compartment and the third compartment is a hopper for holding captured mice. The vaned paddle is clockwork-motivated when wound by a key on the outside of the box. One wind gives fifteen mouse ejections into the hopper. There are openings on each side of the central compartment and the only lure for mice to enter either of these is the cheapest of baits—their curiosity. Once they are inside there is a sensitive pressure plate on the floor and when a mouse treads on it the paddle is sprung into action and the mouse is propelled bodily into the hopper. It follows that it should be possible to catch fifteen mice before the trap has to be reset.

Of course, when mice are caught alive in large numbers, there is still the problem of disposing of them. To provide for this Havahart also supply an accessory drowning bath, so the squeamish are saved the task of taking live mice out of the hopper. The bath is simply a replacement slide lid which has a hose attached to it and this goes into a large glass jar. The jar is filled with water which is meant to attract thirsty mice and this it does, so that they tumble in and are drowned.

The Ketch-All should be placed on the floor so as to allow a gap of not less than 2in (50mm) all around, ensuring that mice have free access to the openings.

Another type of multicatch trap is seen in Figure 18. Although this could be baited (and indeed, if it was thought to be useful, lead-in bait could also be used in the case of the Havahart model) the intention is really, once again, to entice curious mice into the box. This one is constructed from wood and perforated galvanized sheeting and has an entrance hole in one end of the box. There is a hinged lid, held in place when closed by a hook and eye, and the under surface of this lid carries the trapping device. This consists of two funnels of perforated galvanized plate, one leading in horizontally from the hole in the end of the box and, in turn, this is joined to a vertical funnel. While a mouse will squeeze down the second funnel to get into the box, it will find it a different proposition to get back again through the narrow hole in the end. Provided that the trap is visited frequently it will work well and go on taking mice until it is full, but if left unvisited for long it is likely that mice could gnaw their way out. They need only the smallest edge of wood on which to get their teeth working and then escape is no problem. Getting the mice out of the box will need care to avoid losing any. The whole unit could be put into a bucket of water to drown the mice, otherwise they could be gassed by putting the box into a polythene bag linked to a gas generator, as used by public health authorities.

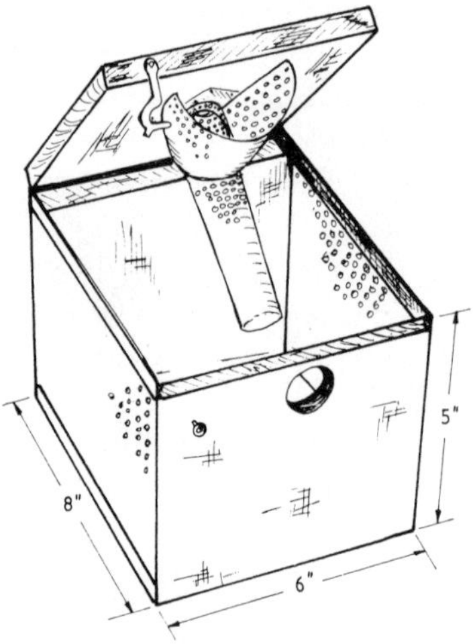

Fig 18 Multicatch mouse trap

Live Traps—Boxes and Cages

This is a group of mammal traps which follows logically from the multicatch mouse traps just described.

In theory, box traps and cage traps can be used to hold any mammal and there have been models produced to catch rhinos, hippos, big cats, antelopes and bears. Regardless of size, the principle involved is basically similar, depending upon a box or cage to hold a live animal as a prisoner, after it has entered through an opening which has a remotely controlled trapdoor. The closing of the door can be operated manually by hidden observers, and this is usually the case with large mammals, or it could be motivated by the captive releasing a trigger and catch system, which has kept the door open. Some doors are non-reversing push-through types.

Before dealing with the kind of box traps which function with a trapdoor, mention should be made of a group of cage traps which have no trapdoor. Generally these are restricted to capturing mice, rats or other small vermin. They are usually made of galvanized wire and tend to be either half-cylindrical in shape, like fish traps, or square in section. They have two compartments and small mammals get into the first through a funnel in the end wall. The dividing wall between the compartments has a non-return push-through door, the principle being that animals can push their way through to get into the second compartment, but as the door is hinged at the top, it falls back under its own weight. Since it overlaps the bottom of the dividing wall it cannot be pushed in the reverse direction. These traps usually have a lockable door in the hutch section through which the catch can be released.

A variation of this type of cage trap is seen on page 101 and is known as the Arouze trap. It differs in the form of the entrance to the second compartment. In the dividing wall there is a funnel which has a flat door and this is formed from a spring-hinged metal flap. When a small mammal goes into the funnel, the flap drops down under its weight and deposits it in the second compartment, but then immediately springs back into place.

These traps are usually baited, always in the second compartment, but sometimes also in the first. Rats and mice as well as stoats and weasels will go into fowl runs and entering a small cage through a funnel requires no greater courage, but the enticement of a suitable bait will overcome any possibility of fear. The baits used for rodents can be those suggested already for mice, but for stoats, weasels and also rats a piece of bacon rind with fat attached will be most attractive. Raw eggs can also be used because all these animals love them. In traps like the Arouze and a similar Havahart model, bait can be put on the flap as an added inducement for an animal to jump on it.

Like steel traps, these cages must be 'seasoned' before being put into use. They can be buried in soil or suspended in a pond to destroy the metallic smell of newness.

The siting of cage traps depends upon the animals to be caught, and field vermin such as stoats and weasels may be more wary than rats, so traps should be camouflaged by covering them with vegetation. In any case it will be as well to disguise them if they are to be left in a public area, if only to prevent them from being damaged or stolen. Usually they do not require to be anchored, although sometimes they have been overturned by an animal captive throwing its weight around in an attempt to escape. Although they are regarded as humane there have been injuries when animals have tried to escape by wrenching the wire framework with their teeth or feet. For this reason it is important that the traps are visited regularly, preferably morning and evening to account for both nocturnal and diurnal animals.

The cage traps more frequently used by trappers are those with a drop door. They come in two varieties: those with a single door and those with a door at each end allowing an apparent run-through or tunnel. These traps are always baited, usually with the bait attached to the trigger which will drop the door into place and close the trap.

An example of the single-door type is the Martin seen in the illustration on page 102. This is a slightly different version from the kinds to be described later, as it has a galvanized iron entrance area with a drop door at one end and a wooden box, providing a protective hutch, at the other. The drop door is operated by a baited treadle inside the cage, so that when an animal steps on the treadle to get at the bait, this releases the door which immediately closes the cage. The wooden hutch is provided with dried grass or straw bedding and a supply of food. It is intended for small vermin up to the size of polecats, martens and skunks. Apart from being a humane trap—the darkened shelter reduces the state of fear felt by captured animals—there is the advantage, as with all live traps, that small domestic animals or rare wild ones can be released unharmed.

There are several other kinds of traps which provide some form of shelter for captives. One of these is the Longworth small-mammal trap, made in Britain and now one of the most popular for scientific research purposes involving experimental work with mice, voles and shrews. It was originally designed by D. H. Chitty and D. A. Kempson of the Bureau of Animal Population at Oxford, and is a two-part trap consisting of a trapping unit and an auxiliary nesting box (see Figure 19).

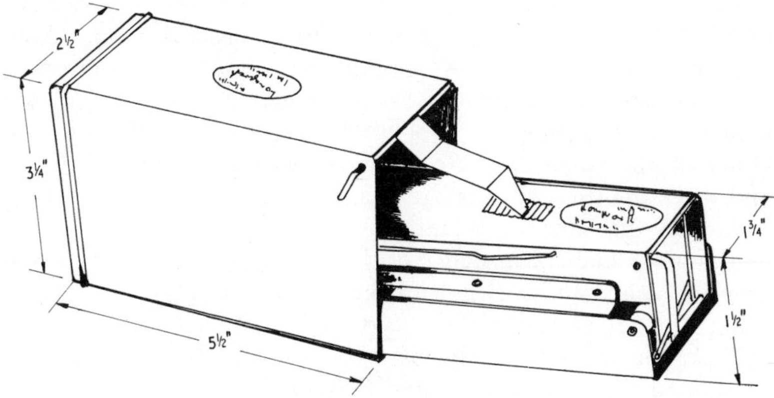

Fig 19 Longworth small mammal trap

The trap is constructed of aluminium alloy and is a nicely engineered piece of equipment allowing for a range of settings that are easily adjusted from very fine to coarse. The penalty for refining a trap to these proportions is its cost which has been rising steadily over the years and is now above £3 ($5.8). But in compensation it is extremely portable as the trap unit can be enclosed within the nesting box and of course its alloy construction reduces its weight to a minimum.

When in use the trap and nest units are in line, locked together with a clip on the nest box which is wedged into one of a series of grooves on the trap unit top, in a kind of ratchet fashion. The whole unit is then 10in (250mm) long, the trap part being $2\frac{3}{8}$in (60mm) wide and $2\frac{1}{8}$in (54mm) high, while the nest box has corresponding measurements of $2\frac{5}{8}$ and $3\frac{3}{8}$in (67 and 86mm). When they are locked, Longworth traps are rigid and strong, so much so that they have been found in a pasture still intact with the occupants unharmed after the unit has been kicked about by cattle.

The nest box is provided with dried grass or strands of sheep wool as nesting material. Sheep wool is very good because its natural oil has very good heat insulation properties and it can easily be gathered from barbed wire fences in sheep pastures. On no account should cotton wool be used, because it will strand and wind around the legs of small mammals and cause considerable discomfort and irritation, if not actual physical injury from tightening like a ligature. As supplied, the nest box has one grave disadvantage. Being metallic its outer surface will collect condensed water during the cool of the night—remembering that many of the small creatures trapped are nocturnal in habit—and when the sun rises next morning the water evaporates taking heat from the metal so that the nest box is converted into a refrigerator. The consequence of this for the small animals inside is very obvious and it is not uncommon to find them dead from cold. The effect can be reduced, if not remedied, either by painting the outside of the nest box with an insulating plastic compound (Pallidux from Liquid Plastics Ltd, Preston, England) or by making a fibreboard insulating cover for the box.

The action of the Longworth trap depends upon an entrance door being kept open by a trigger penetrating through the trap box side wall. The trigger is linked along the outside by a sprung lever which connects with a trip bar inside at the opposite end of the trap box. When an animal is attracted inside the box by bait and moves towards the nest box, it trips over the bar and the door closes, with a locking bar dropping to seal the door on the outside. There is an additional pre-baiting clamping device which prevents the door from being closed even if the bar inside is tripped. In experimental situations where large-scale trapping is taking place on a grid pattern to check a population, for example, the overall result can be improved if the traps are pre-baited for several days before the trapping mechanisms are set.

The traps can be set in animal runs under hedgerows, along rocky ledges, within woods, under a shrub layer and also in grass. Being small they are easily camouflaged, and this is most important, because being made of shiny metal they can reflect sunlight to look like a signalling lamp. They are baited with cereals including crushed oats or oatmeal, rolled wheat or barley and flour, with some used as a lead-in and a plentiful supply inside the nest box. Traps must be visited morning and evening at least.

There is a knack for releasing captives, but although this is easy to demonstrate it is difficult to describe. There is no problem, however, if the whole trap and nest unit is put into a deep polythene bag before the components are separated and the captives released. When scientific surveys are being carried out the animals are measured, sexed and generally examined for external parasites before being released again. Sometimes they are marked by toe clipping, ear tattooing or fur dyeing so that they can be recognized if they are recaptured, thus preventing flaws in any statistics being compiled.

A similar type of trap used in New Zealand has been described by R. L. Edgar in the *Journal of Mammalogy*. An exploded diagram of this is seen in Figure 20, but full details of the construction are given by Edgar. It combines all of the functions of the Longworth trap, including the regulation of the setting, pre-baiting and protection for the captives, but it has one clear advantage in being collapsible. The diagram shows metal lugs (a) which grip the base and the roof to the sides and the whole is fastened

Fig 20 Edgar trap

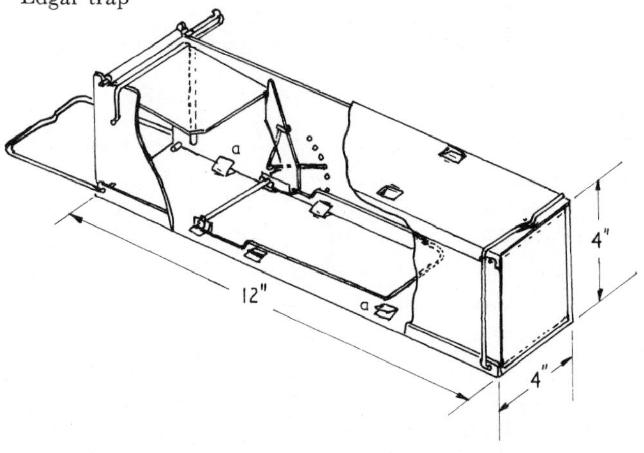

together with pivoted wire clips on each end. The maker claims that the 11.8 by 3.9in (300 by 100mm) square trap can be folded down to a pack 12.6 by 3.9 by 1.6in (320 by 100 by 40mm) and weighing 24oz (680g). The main difference in the operation of the Longworth and the Edgar trap is the use by the latter of a wire treadle instead of a trip wire to close the door. The larger size allows the trap to capture animals as big as stoats and hedgehogs.

A single-door trap with a variation is the whole family rat trap, seen on page 102. It is made from galvanized wire and a simple door is hinged at one end so that when opened it can be tipped up over the top of the cage. It fits under a bar to which is attached the rod-catch and this goes over the door to keep it horizontal. It is finely set against a loop of wire extended from the bait trigger inside the cage. If the bait lever has some bacon fat attached to it, a rat entering through the open door will close this when it pulls at the bait. At the opposite end of the cage is a flap-up door hinged at the top and while this is too small to allow an adult rat to enter, it would allow young ones through. The intention and hope is that if a female rat which has left a litter of young in a nest is trapped and cries for the young, they will respond by coming in search of her. They enter through the flap door—hence the name for the trap.

To be successful, a trap of this kind must be sited in a position likely to be close to a rat's nest. Where rat infestations are heavy, this is not too difficult to establish, for while it may not always be possible to see the nests, the squeaks of the young can often be heard. Careful observation may also indicate the places to which adult rats are taking food.

Squirrel Traps

The pestilent nature of grey squirrels in Britain, particularly in plantations and forest nurseries, has required that extensive control measures are undertaken. Squirrels can be captured with the use of spring traps, but this could be a dangerous practice in those areas where the introduced North American grey squirrel is living side by side with the indigenous British red form, which is being conserved, and for this reason cage traps are preferred. A series called Legg squirrel traps has been developed and approved by the Forestry Commission and the Ministry of Agriculture, Fisheries and Food.

There are three versions, the Legg PB (permanently baited) Trap, the Legg Midget and the Legg Single-Catch Trap.

The Single-Catch is really a conventional wire-cage trap having a drop door. There is a treadle at the back of the cage and when this is depressed it releases a ring, peg and wire link to the door which falls under its own weight. The trap can be pre-baited by lifting the door out of its guides and leaving it on the top of the cage. There is a door in the back through which a captive squirrel can be removed. Trapping sites must be level otherwise the door will not drop smoothly. The door guides must also be kept clean and free from debris. The trap can be anchored with pegs or held down with rocks or logs.

These traps require inspection from time to time as squirrels do gnaw and weaken both the wire-mesh of the body of the cage and also the trip wire.

The Legg PB (illustrated on page 68) and the Midget (see Figure 21) are alike in using swing doors through which the squirrels enter. The Midget is a small version of the PB and is designed for single-catch use in gardens.

The PB is a large cage trap consisting of a central tunnel with a 41in (105mm) square entrance, which leads to a pair of hutches, one on either side, for retaining captive squirrels. The tunnel is entered through two swing doors, one behind the other, and these are at an angle so that after a squirrel has pushed through they will fall back under their own weight. Two metal baffles, one

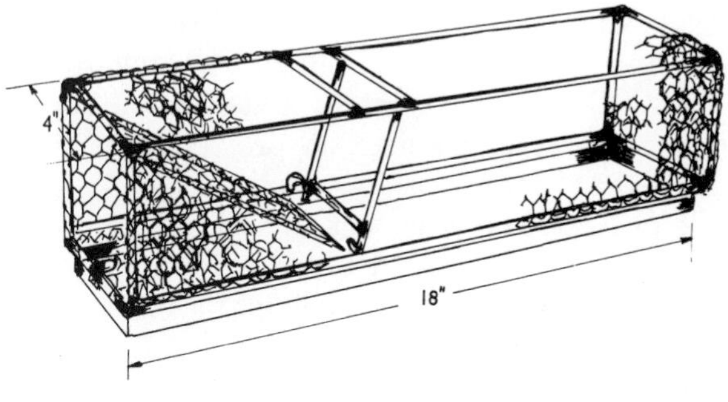

Fig 21 Legg Midget trap

behind each door, prevent the squirrels from opening the doors from inside. The sides of the tunnel are of solid metal and the fronts of the hutches also have solid metal doors, so that an incoming squirrel cannot see the captives in the hutches. The doors in the hutches allow for removing the captives.

Under the tunnel of the PB and also under the Midget, there is a detachable metal bait tray which is fitted so that the wire-mesh floor of the cage is above it.

On site, both traps should be buried so that the bait trays are level with the ground surface and the traps are preferably pegged down, or held with pieces of timber. Pre-baiting is advisable if a large catch is desired and this is accomplished by pegging the swing doors open and taking the hutch doors out for a few days. Only minimum maintenance is necessary for the traps, but oiling is useful to ensure that the swing doors move easily, and the trap should be inspected regularly for damage by the gnawing rodents. Unused traps should be turned upside down on site to prevent the capture of squirrels which would not be discovered during an absence of inspections.

Grey squirrels are mainly active during the day, particularly just after sunrise or immediately before sunset, and although they are tree-dwellers by habit—their nests or dreys are a good indication of their presence—they spend a lot of their time foraging on the ground. None the less, they are seldom far away from trees, preferably oak or beech, but other deciduous trees and even conifers are sometimes used. They are very rapid movers and to see them in the open it may be necessary to remain motionless in a wood for some time.

Squirrel damage, such as peeled bark from deciduous trees, chewed-off shoots and buds, chewed fruit in orchards, attacks on peas and beans in market gardens and pheasant and partridge eggs taken from estate hatcheries, all provide clues for trap sites.

Bait can include soaked yellow maize seeds or wheat seeds, sliced apple or pear, and beef suet. If yellow maize is left about and the germ is taken, leaving the husk behind, this is a sure sign of squirrels. Mice will chew the whole grain, but leave fragments about, and birds will take the whole lot away.

Multicatch traps must be visited once a day and the single-catch traps preferably twice a day. Squirrels can deliver a pretty fierce bite and therefore care should be taken in dealing with captives. They are best removed from traps by placing a sack over the entrance and encouraging them to run into it. This can be assisted by putting the trap and sack on to a slope, the sack uppermost as the animals will move upwards in preference to downwards. Once they are inside the sack they should be urged into a corner where they can easily be killed by a sharp blow to the head.

See-Saw Trap

An early example of this type to be used in Britain was the Whitlock Weasel Trap (King 1973), but this is no longer commercially available. However, a model known as the Clausius trap, which is based upon a wooden box trap used over many years on the European mainland, is available and used extensively for taking small vermin alive. It measures 2ft (610mm) in length and has one end 5 by 4in (125 by 100mm) and the other 4in (100mm) square. Thus it has a sloping top. The smaller end is open as an entrance, the other end has either a wire-mesh covering or else a sheet of glass or Perspex. Inside there is a wooden platform which is pivoted so that the part that is nearer to the trap entrance is slightly longer than the other and will, when the trap is in position, slope downwards towards the entrance. Also, under this longer section is hinged a three-sided piece of wire, the two ends of which are sharpened to points. When an animal enters the trap, stimulated by bait at the other end, it mounts the platform and as it reaches just beyond the centre point this tilts downwards towards the closed end. At the same time the hinged wire drops down and the points dig into the wooden base of the trap. Thus, even if the animal backs up against the platform, there is no chance of this reversing the tilt and allowing it to escape. (See page 119.)

These traps can be used for a wide range of animals, especially stoats, weasels and rats. They may be sited in all manner of situations, such as by boundary walls, among stacks of wood, in hedgerows and beside streams. The glass or Perspex-ended type can be used to great effect in the middle of a plank, preferably no wider than the trap, stretched over a small stream, for as an animal can see through the 'tunnel' it will attempt to use it as a passageway to cross the water. Where there is a stone wall from which a few stones can be removed at the base, the traps can be used side by side in pairs, pointing in opposite directions. They should be left in place for several days, even if they have made a capture, because these animals tend to live in small communities and so where there is one there are likely to be others.

Mink Traps

The spread of feral mink, which since 1929 have been escaping from fur-farms in Britain, has now covered most of the river systems. They have successfully adapted themselves to the countryside and bred to produce natural colonies. The animal is a pest on several counts, being no friend of the angler because of the way it can deplete the stocks of fish in rivers; it also attacks domestic poultry, arouses animosity in gamekeepers when it attacks gamebirds, and the owners of ornamental waterfowl find that it is no friend to them either.

North America is the natural home of the mink and in the wild they feed on a wide range of prey, many forms of which would be seen as vermin, so that they are not regarded as pests in the same way that they are in Britain. They will devour insects, crayfish, fish, frogs, birds, mice, ground squirrels, cottontail rabbits and muskrats. In Britain, the absence of large numbers of some of these sources of food has inevitably meant that the mink must look elsewhere.

In an attempt to control feral mink, the Ministry of Agriculture, Fisheries and Food has undertaken large-scale trapping and has developed a special cage trap for the purpose. As seen in the illustration on page 119, it is a square-ended trap with a covering of square wire-mesh. At one end there is a hinged solid metal door and this is set in a raised position, held by a catch linked to a bait lever. These traps are usually baited with fish and placed among vegetation debris on a river bank.

Fox Traps

When it became illegal in England and Wales to use gin traps in 1958, and when the same restriction was extended to Scotland in 1973, there was widespread alarm among gamekeepers and

A goshawk trap (*Philip Glasier*)

The Lloyd spring trap

A two-piece tunnel trap using an Imbra (*Forestry Commission*)

A Legg PB trap

farmers because of the effect this might have upon the war they waged on foxes. They could still be hunted with hounds, they could be gassed or shot, but gassing cannot be undertaken indiscriminately and the other controls take both time and manpower. Unfortunately at that time there were no humane spring traps sufficiently powerful to kill a fox. The Conibear 330, used as a trail-set trap, could take a fox, but of course equally well it could take domestic and rare wild animals and its use in a tunnel would be difficult to arrange.

The remedy seemed to be a cage trap and one of the more successful of these is the Hunter designed by Mr C. Howell of Cheshire. It is a large, heavy-gauge and square-mesh wire trap and for a fox it has nothing much to distinguish it from a poultry run. It is baited with a dead fowl or with offal, and it is securely pegged to the ground, either, as shown on page 120, in a situation like a stockyard, or in open country. The bait is placed on a central pan running the width of the trap and this activates the closure of the door. In trials using this trap, it has proved successful in capturing foxes, but it is bulky, obviously not cheap to buy and used as a single unit in fox-infested country it is limited in its power to serve as a control measure.

Run-through Traps

These traps are fundamentally the same in function and action as the single drop-door box and cage traps. The differences are the presence of two doors, one at each end, and the philosophy of encouraging timid animals during a pre-baiting stage to treat the trap as a tunnel with free access to run through. Like all traps, this includes an element of subterfuge.

A wide range of these traps have been produced and one may expect even more to appear as a result of public opinion coming down heavily in favour of humane and selective trapping.

There are two main areas of variation among the existing traps. There are those which provide a covered roof, thereby giving protection to captured animals from the effects of exposure to sun or rain. Some have a trigger and release catch mechanism on the top of the trap and others have it on the side. If it is on the side, there is less chance of it being accidentally released by falling debris, or of it jamming when the trap is camouflaged.

Some other features which are considered undesirable in cage traps are solid bottoms which prevent animal urine or rainwater from draining away, and spring-activated doors, which can be ineffective when the springs have become weakened with frequent use and allow captive animals to push their way out again.

Among the better traps in this category are those in the Havahart range. Although they are manufactured in the United States a good many are imported into Britain and, indeed, to countries throughout the world. In their favour is good construction, simple operation and freedom from the major faults already listed. They can be used in a variety of situations as they allow for pre-baiting, use as a single-door trap and as a run-through type. One valuable feature is the presence of wire stays above the doors, so designed that when the doors close the stays drop down and slot into projecting lugs above the doors. This is an automatic locking device which prevents prisoners from pushing out through the doors to escape but has none of the wear and tear defects of the springs meant to serve the same purpose in other kinds of traps.

When the trap has taken an animal, not only is the whole top covered with galvanized sheet metal, but the doors of the same material are now sloping downwards at each end (see the picture on page 120) providing an adequate run-off for rainwater. The catches run from the door hinges, outside the cage and interconnect with a trigger attached to a pivoted metal bait treadle inside. The contact trigger and catch is such that a very fine and delicate setting adjustment is possible, although it is perfectly easy to use the trap with a coarse setting if desired.

If the trap is to be used in conjunction with a burrow, its open end is placed at the mouth and the end with the door closed faces outwards. The catch lever of the closed door is simply moved out of contact with the trigger. Rocks or logs should be arranged around the hole and trap mouth so that an emerging animal must either back into the burrow or enter the trap. If a suitable bait is used the animal should enter the trap without any further problem. Ensure that other burrows of the system are also blocked so that they cannot be used as escape holes.

The Havahart No 2 can be used for muskrats where they are working beside water and it should be sited among logs and bushes. It measures 24in (610mm) by 7in (180mm) square and as a one end set it can be used for all but the larger squirrels.

The Havahart No 6 is designed especially for mink, so that it can operate when submerged under water. It has a hook for attaching fish bait, instead of using a treadle. Pre-baited for a few days before the trapping season begins and secured so that it cannot be sprung, it will allow mink to familiarize themselves with it and ensure catches from the beginning when it is set.

The smallest trap in the Havahart range is the No 0 which measures 10in (255mm) long by 3in (75mm) square. It is intended for shrews, voles and mice, and where climatic conditions allow for exposure of these animals, its run-through feature probably gives it an edge over the Longworth trap.

The two biggest Havahart traps are the No 3 and the 3A, the first being 36in (915mm) long and 11in (280mm) square, while the second is 42in (1.07m) long and 11 by 13in (280 by 330mm). The No 3 is recommended for racoons, opossums, cats, woodchucks and jackrabbits, while the larger should be used for nutria, large racoons and bobcats.

Racoons are caught readily in these traps when they are employed in a one-end set. This is improved if the bait pan has a wooden block placed underneath at the open-door end, to ensure that the racoon moves over the centre line before springing the door. This guarantees that the animal is completely inside, otherwise a long one will keep the door open with its back, get the bait and then back out to escape with a free meal. For preference the bait should be placed at the end with the closed door and protected above with planks of wood to prevent the racoon from reaching through the wire mesh to get it. Smoked fish is recommended for both 'coons and 'possums, as it has a penetrating odour and does not go off too quickly.

There is a variety of baits for use with box and cage traps, depending upon the animals to be trapped. Muskrats, nutria and opossums can be attracted with fruit and vegetables. Nutria are fond of bananas and melons and although muskrats will take apples they probably prefer root vegetables such as carrots, parsnips and turnips. Opossums will also respond to apples as well as fresh vegetables, but they have quite catholic tastes and will find sardines and bacon fat irresistible.

Foxes and muskrats can be attracted with musk scent from their own kind—a trapper who regularly catches these animals might be a source for this.

Bobcats, wild and feral cats can easily be enticed with fish and offal, as can mink and otters. Gophers are fond of a mixture of molasses and peanut butter and this can be spread on brown bread for attachment to a trap.

Stoats and weasels will enter traps baited with offal, especially liver, but chicken entrails are also effective and can be used for skunks as well.

Chipmunks are fond of all kinds of seeds, including those from sunflowers, maize, wheat and oats, but in common with many other animals they readily respond to oil of anise soaked into bread. Much the same range of baits can be used for squirrels.

It may be a problem to dispose of animals from live traps if they have to be killed humanely. The sack method already described for squirrels can be used with the larger mammals, and it is always possible to shoot them. Chloroform can be used in a polythene bag, but on no account should ether be used because of its explosive property. Carbon dioxide gas can be used at a strength of 10 per cent to narcotize and increased to 50 to 60 per cent to anaesthetize and then eventually asphyxiate.

Crush Traps

The last of the mammal traps to be described is one used for capturing antelopes, but it could also be used for most types of animals which live in herds, including deer and zebra.

This is by far the largest of traps and can only be compared with the large decoys used for wildfowl.

The principle of the trap is to provide an enclosure into which animals can be herded. It could be done by beaters driving towards the trap, but on a large scale a helicopter is found to be most effective. The structure, as seen in Figure 22, has a fence enclosing a square of ground, each side being up to 150yd (137m) in length. The fence can be of nylon mesh and should be at least 4ft (1.2m) high. The mesh should be fitted so that any side can be opened by letting it down, with the attachment only remaining at the bottom. The side to be opened can be varied according to the direction from which the herd will approach.

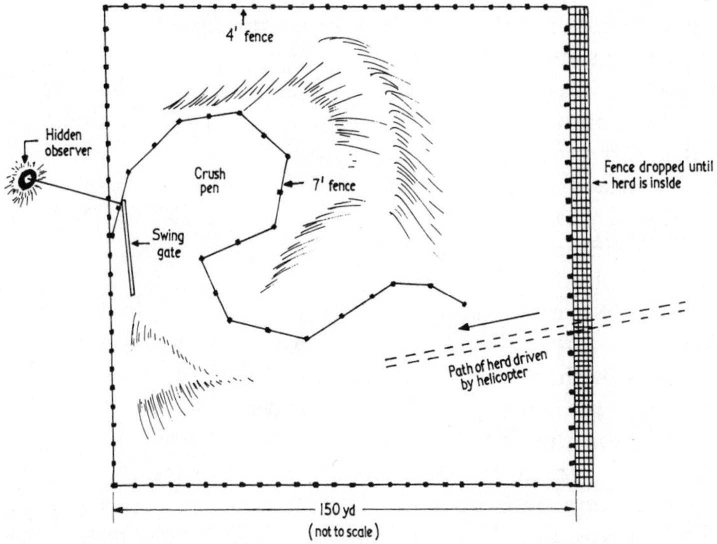

Fig 22 Colorado crush trap

The trap should be sited as naturally as possible, preferably with a surrounding of trees and bush cover to break up the outline. If there is a natural fence with which animals are familiar this could be incorporated.

Inside the enclosure is a crush fence and catch pen, the latter with a swing gate controlled by someone concealed at a distance out of sight. The fencing here should be at least 7ft (2.1m) high.

Before a herd is moved towards the enclosure, a number of people conceal themselves outside in order to be in a position to erect the dropped mesh fencing once the animals are inside. The helicopter pilot will discover by trial and error whether his machine, its noise or its shadow are effective in moving a herd, but once he has manoeuvred the herd into the trap, he has to hover to keep them there until the fencing is closed. In this respect it is rather like a shepherd and sheepdog herding sheep.

With the herd inside the trap all is left for a day or two in order to give the animals a chance to settle down; then men will urge them towards the crush fence and when all are inside the gate is closed by the hidden observer. After another day or so without disturbance, the animals are captured individually and placed in vehicles for transportation.

This trap was originally designed by the Colorado State Fish and Game Department, but variations of it have entered service in Africa, South America and Australia.

Legislation

Britain

The Pests Act of 1954 made it illegal after 31 July 1959 to use any trap in England and Wales not approved as humane by the Ministry of Agriculture, Fisheries and Food. The use of leg-hold steel traps (gins) was permitted, for foxes only, in Scotland until 1 April 1973. In Northern Ireland the leg-hold trap became illegal on 1 January 1969. Despite this legislation it is still legal to manufacture steel leg-hold traps in Britain for export.

The Badger Act 1973 gave legal protection to badgers, except where, for agricultural purposes, they could be considered as pests.

The Conservation of Wild Creatures and Wild Plants Act 1975 gives protection to rare species in Britain. Included are two bats, the mouse-eared and the greater horseshoe, which the Act says cannot be taken, injured, killed, sold or offered for sale. Similarly the bats cannot, except under licence, be ringed (banded).

The Endangered Species (Import and Export) Act 1976, lists the animals which can be exploited. Like similar legislation in Gambia and Sweden any other creatures are 'off limits'.

From 1977 the otter has received similar protection to that received by the badger, mainly owing to pressure from conservationists alarmed at the apparent decline in otter numbers.

Europe

On the European mainland a number of countries have for a long time had legislation outlawing the leg-hold trap. The earliest was Denmark in 1931, followed by Norway in 1932 and Germany in 1933. In West Germany (although the law was relaxed during the last war) it is now illegal to sell leg-hold traps. In Austria the leg-hold trap is reckoned generally to have been illegal since 1938, but some of the provinces allow its use under local laws. Switzerland made the trap illegal in 1962, but owing to the spread of rabies by foxes, these are allowed to be killed by using steel traps.

Box traps are allowed in Denmark and for weasels in Austria where humane killing traps can be used for polecats, foxes and martens.

In France, animals classed as game may not be taken with leg-hold traps; included are hares, deer, rabbits and wild boar. These traps can be used for pests nominated by Department Prefects, but the sites used and the number set must be notified to the appropriate municipal authority.

Leg-hold trapping of classified pests is permitted in Italy, providing that the traps are inspected one hour before sunrise and one hour after sunset.

There are no legal restraints for using leg-hold traps in Spain, Portugal and Luxembourg.

Occupiers of land in Holland may obtain permission from the police to use leg-hold traps within their own curtilage, but other people require a Ministry of Agriculture Licence. Under a law which became effective in July 1977 there can be a punishment of up to three months' imprisonment or a fine of up to 1,000 guilders for persons who sell exotic species, dead or alive.

Traps that kill can be used in Norway, although the distinction between some of these and leg-hold traps is difficult to establish.

In Sweden fur-bearers, including polecats, martens, mink and foxes can be captured in box traps, most of which are heavy, wooden-slatted constructions. The traps must be visited daily. Leg-hold traps may be set, under licence, according to the revision of the Game Protection Acts in 1965, for taking otter and mink in order to protect fish in breeding areas.

In Finland bear trapping is illegal, but mink and muskrat may be trapped, the latter in drowning sets. Traps must be inspected daily.

Cage traps are used in West Germany, but they must be inspected daily. The see-saw trap is very popular for small vermin.

Quick-killing traps are permitted in Yugoslavia, subject to legislation controlling the close seasons for hunting. There is similar legislation in the Soviet Union, although here leg-hold traps are permitted in the open season.

North America

In the United States there is some Federal legislation but, by and large, trapping regulations are enforced on a state-by-state basis.

In states where fur-bearers are trapped it is the usual practice to conserve by legislation for close seasons, sometimes imposing bag limits and licensing trappers. It is considered that there are now relatively few full-time professional trappers in the United States, but an increasing number of people are operating their trap lines in their spare time, particularly schoolboys. Oddly, schoolchildren do not require a licence in many states, and where they do require one it may be supplied at a reduced fee.

Since 1967 bears have been protected in California from being taken in leg-hold traps, but bear trapping is illegal in Arizona and restricted in Wisconsin and Michigan.

The states of Wisconsin, New York and New Jersey have made the use of pole traps illegal.

In 1971 the use of steel traps in counties with heavy populations was banned by the state of Alabama, although a legislative loophole allows people to trap within the boundaries of their residences.

As long ago as 1927 steel leg-hold traps were made illegal in South Carolina, except within 200yd (184m) of a residence or fowlhouse. The sale or manufacture of these traps within the state was also banned.

The general use of steel traps has been banned in the state of Florida by its Game and Freshwater Fish Commission. This legislation, which came into force on 1 January 1973, is quite exceptional as it applies not only to leg-hold traps, but also to humane killer traps. The only exception is for farmers who may protect their property by setting out not more than five steel traps. Steel traps were banned in Maine in 1969 and in Massachusetts they can only be used with a jaw length less than 5½in (140mm).

New Jersey, the most densely populated state, enacted legislation in 1972 which bans all leg-hold trapping in the most heavily populated counties. This covers about half of the state. Leg-hold trapping by persons under the age of fourteen is banned everywhere and trapping is not allowed without a licence. Since February 1969, ten municipalities have introduced ordinances which either ban trapping or restrict it.

Apart from the above legislation and a requirement in fifteen states that traps must be inspected daily, there is little effective control and even the effectiveness of requiring daily inspections depends upon enforcement.

Detailed information about state legislation can be obtained from the Fish and Game Commissions or from the State Directors and the addresses of these will be found in the *Conservation Directory* obtainable from the National Wildlife Federation, 1412, 16th Street, NW, Washington DC, 20036.

There is increasing pressure in the United States from conservation bodies to ban the use of steel traps throughout and it is likely that new legislation will appear on a more regular basis.

On 3 March 1973, a Convention on International Trade in Endangered Species of Wild Flora and Fauna (CITES) was signed by twenty-one countries in Washington and soon after a further fifteen signatures were received. Now the total has reached forty-one. The Convention provides for control in the trade of listed animals and plants, including a number of fur-bearers, by the necessity for permits which authorize the export or import of species. The permits must declare that scientific authorities do not consider the export of a species will endanger its continued existence in the country of origin. The significance of this Convention, if ratified by all the signatories, would be to discourage trapping for commercial gain in respect of the species listed.

At the moment the regulations are relaxed in Britain in respect of a limited list of scientific institutions nominated by the British government as the managing authority. These institutions are issued with an open licence.

Canada

Regulations concerning trapping are issued on a provincial basis, except that they do not apply to Indians who are under the jurisdiction of the Federal Department of Indian Affairs and Northern Development. It so happens that in some provinces most of the trappers are Indians and therefore unlicensed. Otherwise, trappers in the majority of provinces require a licence and trapping is regulated by the operation of close seasons. Usually only a provincial resident can obtain a licence, although some provinces operate a reciprocal agreement.

In some provinces, farmers and landowners trapping on their own property do not require a licence, although they often need permission to trap and have to supply reports of their captures.

Trappers are often restricted to a particular area and are encouraged to use short trap lines in order to ensure regular inspection, unless of course snowmobiles are used. Trapping is not allowed on Crown land or in National Parks except for special provisions granted by the Lieutenant-Governor in Council.

Bears, but not polar bears, may be trapped in all provinces except for British Columbia.

The Government of Newfoundland and Labrador has banned, under the Beaver Trapping Order 1971/1972, the use of leg-hold traps in the designated Beaver Management Areas 1, 2 and 5.

The use of Conibear traps is being encouraged in Canada especially at trapper training courses and although the use of pole traps is not illegal, their use is discouraged.

Chile

In 1970 it became illegal to possess, use, manufacture, sell or transport leg-hold traps.

Mexico

Trapping requires a licence.

New Zealand

There are two pests for which control measures include the use of leg-hold traps; these are rabbits and opossums. The Rabbit Amendment Act 1957 made it illegal to export or sell the skins and carcases of rabbits, so that there was no inducement to encourage breeding. Instead, attempts have been made to reduce their numbers through the activities of pest destruction boards.

In New Zealand, opossums have spread throughout the country to an extent where it is no longer considered possible to exercise control on a national basis. Instead, pest control measures which include the use of leg-hold traps are concentrated in areas where numbers reach pest proportions. Although pole traps are illegal, pole snares and ground snares are used extensively. Traps must be inspected daily.

Australia

Legislation for animal protection is a state responsibility, although in 1973 a federal ban was imposed on the exporting of the skins and meat of kangaroos. These are the animals for which most control exists.

Rabbit trapping is universally practised without any restriction, but it is only one of the control measures which also include the use of poison gases and baits.

Opossums may be taken in Tasmania, but only with the use of snares, which must be inspected every thirty-six hours. The opossum is protected in New South Wales.

In the state of Victoria the Vermin and Noxious Weed Destruction Board now has twenty full-time trappers concerned with the control of feral dogs and cats, dingoes and foxes.

2 Trapping Birds

A growing conviction is spreading throughout the world that killing birds is rarely justifiable. Taking birds alive, while condoned in some instances, is also frowned upon, especially if the reason is for trading. It is true that there is still a market for live birds, in some parts of the world more than others, with songbirds and brightly coloured tropical birds being sought in particular. But many people will argue that to keep any birds in cages will cause them distress, even if they have been bred in captivity.

At the present time a huge annual toll is taken of birds migrating between Africa and Europe, with the greatest pressure being at their resting points, such as Cyprus. Similarly in Italy and France birds are shot or trapped in millions each year to supply delicacies for the table—tiny birds such as blackcap warblers, robins, lesser whitethroats, skylarks and various finches.

In Britain legislation prevents this happening and also forbids the importation of wild birds killed elsewhere. Other European countries are beginning to take some notice and in 1971 Belgium—where until then 15 million small birds each year were estimated killed for the table or live-trapped for sale to cagebird enthusiasts—introduced a ban on trapping. Unfortunately, under pressure from the bird-catching interest, the Belgian Government relaxed its ban and, for example, allowed a bag of 120,000 in the autumn of 1973.

There are, in fact, some legitimate occasions when trapping birds can be justified. Some birds in certain circumstances can be considered as pests, and even in Britain with its strong legal provisions, some bird trapping is considered permissible. Examples of bird pests are pigeons, especially the feral pigeons found in large conurbations, crows and some other members of the corvid family, and also domestic sparrows and starlings which can reach plague proportions. In fruit-growing areas bullfinches are considered pests and British fruit growers are allowed to catch them. There are times when gamekeepers wish to live-trap pheasants, not because they are pests, but in order to capture some breeding stock to increase the birds on an estate or for a syndicate.

It is also legitimate to live-trap birds for scientific purposes, usually for ringing (banding in the United States), placing small, lightweight bands, carrying coded identification symbols, on their legs. In Britain bird ringers are licensed and they use various forms of traps. When ringed birds are recovered some time later, perhaps not too far away from where the ringing was carried out, or maybe hundreds if not thousands of miles away, the rings help scientists to unravel their movements. Sometimes this gives a clue to the spread of bird-carried parasites or disease-causing viruses.

Presumably, while it is still possible to acquire licences for importing birds for zoological gardens and so-called wild-bird sanctuaries, there will be a use for traps with which to take them.

A more laudable reason for trapping birds might be to build up a breeding stock of rarities, especially if there is a threat of extinction. This has been achieved at the Wildfowl Trust at Slimbridge, England, where Sir Peter Scott and his team of ornithologists have bred the near-extinct Nene or Hawaiian goose to a point where it could be re-established in its native land. At the Trust there is a decoy which is used to gather in wildfowl arriving after migration and to check the birds scientifically as well as marking them.

Cage Traps

These are relatively small traps which are used to capture birds up to crow or pheasant size. They are usually portable and can be used for pest control on a small scale or for capturing single birds for ringing. While they can be home-made there is a wide range available from trap manufacturers and these may include a number of novel features for attracting birds and also for functioning automatically. Most are made of wire-mesh fastened over thick wire or iron-rod frames. The better ones are galvanized to withstand wet and to avoid rusting; sometimes, however, a frustrated captive may peck at the wire and remove the galvanized finish.

To be effective a cage trap will usually require baiting to attract a bird, the type of bait depending upon the bird wanted. The way into a cage trap may be through a funnel entrance, similar to the funnels used in fish traps, or there may be automatically closing doors which are released when a bait pan inside the trap is agitated. The funnel traps can be multicatchers and it is possible that once birds have entered they will serve as decoys for others. The trap-door-type cages will usually only make single catches, although occasionally more than one bird is found inside, presumably when an earlier occupant has failed to use sufficient pressure on a not too finely set tripping device.

The placing of cage traps is important and this will be assisted by a good knowledge of bird habits, including the kind of food that they eat, where they are commonly to be found and whether they are solitary or flocking by nature.

Fig 23 Bird traps on the approach to a crop

For catching ground-feeding birds such as pigeons, pheasants, partridges, quail and guinea fowl, especially if this is to protect crops, a watch should be kept if possible to find the route they are likely to follow when visiting the planted area. If there is cover nearby, such as hedgerows or plantations, or if there are spaces between rows of plants such as cabbages or kale, these are the likely paths that they will take. Sometimes they will enter a field of a sprouting cereal crop having approached through a ride in a wood. Traps can be positioned on any of these routes with the hope of catching the birds before they get too far into a crop. As long as the traps are suitably baited there is no need to camouflage them, because the greed of these birds will overcome any fear that they might have (see Figure 23). The best baits to use are soaked grains such as maize, barley or wheat, and they will be even more effective if they have been allowed to sprout. A few grains can also be scattered outside the traps as a lead-in through the doors or funnel entrances. It is most important to realize that the traps must be visited several times a day to prevent captive birds from suffering, especially if the traps are in the open and exposed to either sun or rain. It is also possible that birds of other kinds will be caught and they must be promptly released.

One of the simplest bird traps is a cage trap operated manually. This has a door hinged across the top, held open by a stick or piece of wire to which a piece of string is attached. The string is trailed behind some form of cover, such as bushes, where the operator hides. As long as the operator can see what is going on, without being seen himself, there is no problem. Of course the traps must be baited and as soon as a bird has entered the trap the string must be pulled to remove the prop stick and close the door.

Cage traps can of course be built to the size appropriate for the birds to be caught.

Pigeon traps are usually multicatch traps and also self-setting. A trap such as the Havahart No 9, which measures 24 by 18 by 8in (610 by 457 by 203mm), will catch up to ten pigeons. The principle is to have a door in the end or side of the trap, hinged across the top so that it can only swing inwards. The bars at the bottom of the trap-door overlap the wire frame at the bottom

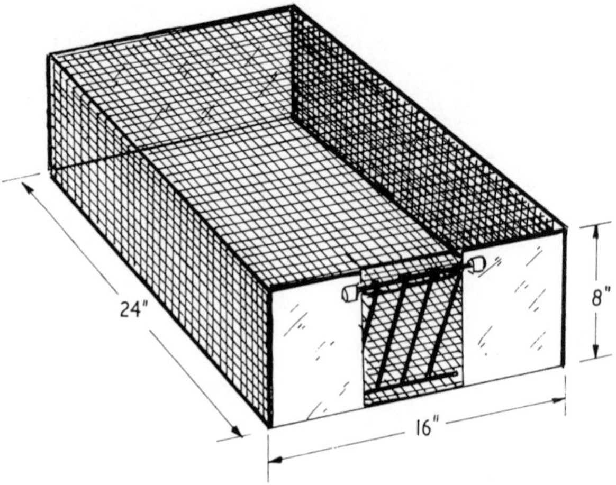

Fig 24 Havahart No. 9 pigeon trap

inside edge of the cage. The pigeons are attracted by a suitable bait, such as soaked corn or proprietory pigeon food and they push their way through the door and into the trap. Of course they cannot escape because of the one-way door system (see Figure 24). Plenty of bait must be provided for multicatching pigeons because they have huge appetites. There is little need to worry about the siting of pigeon traps, other than to place them in an area where the birds congregate. If they are pests in the garden or house yard, this is where to put traps. Anything else which finds its way into the trap, such as a house kitten or pup or another kind of bird, can be released.

Pigeons which are to be destroyed can be humanely killed in a variety of ways suitable for most birds. Pentobarbitone sodium solution is a material used by veterinarians and a few millilitres injected into a bird from a hypodermic syringe (preferably a pre-filled cartridge type) will kill rapidly and painlessly. Most birds can be killed humanely by the application of pressure on the breastbone, which is located behind the breast just above the legs. The action compresses the lungs and stops the heart.

The Potter trap is an automatic type designed to catch single birds from pigeon size downwards. The door slides on a framework which is continued above one end of the trap cage. When pushed to its limit it is held in place by a lever bar from a pivoted trip pan. The bait can be wild-bird food obtained from commercial suppliers and is placed within the cage beyond the trip pan so that birds moving over the pan to get it release the door which slides down its frame to cut off their retreat (see Figure 25).

Figure 26 shows the Chardonneret trap, which, as the translation of its French name implies, was designed to trap goldfinches, although it could trap any finches and may also be adapted to take warblers. The important difference between this trap and those previously described is that it is designed for small perching birds which are seldom, if ever, ground feeders. The trapping feature is a door prop which is released when a bird drops on to a perch supporting it and the opened door. Suitable

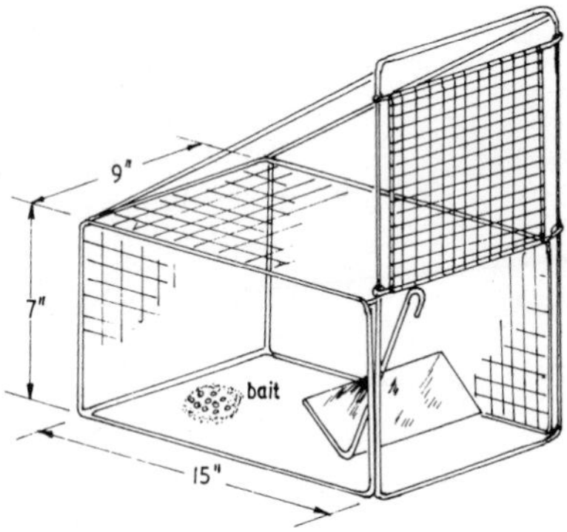

Fig 25 Potter automatic bird trap

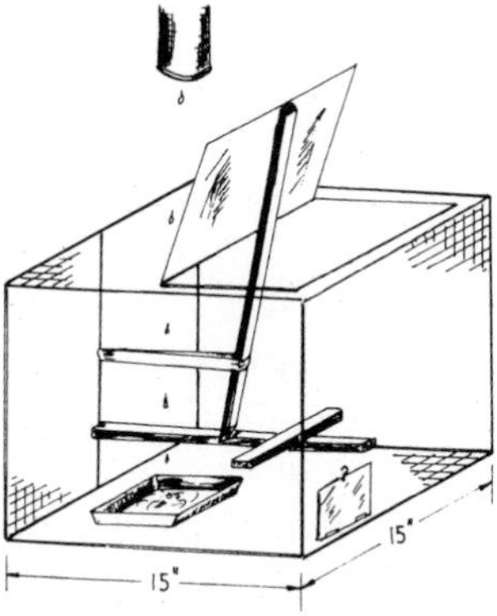

Fig 26 Chardonneret trap

baits can be placed in the cage to attract finches and while bunches of millet seed can be effective, fruit such as chopped apple or sticks of conserved figs will be even better.

A can with a small hole pierced in the bottom and filled with water is suspended above the trap to attract warblers. A drip can is placed in the bottom of the trap to catch the drops of water as they fall from above and of course this produces splashing. Normally warblers are shy and retiring birds, but the dripping and splashing water seems to exert a compelling attraction which overcomes their fear.

Because perching birds such as finches and warblers are easily frightened, the trap should be made as unobtrusive as possible. Its wire-mesh covering should be painted a drab green or brown colour to blend with the ground or with shrubbery. As the bottom of the cage is made of mesh, this allows small plants or grass to poke through to give a natural appearance. Warblers will never fly straight into a trap, but will approach it flying from one patch of cover to another until they are quite close. For this reason the trap must be placed among the bushes and can also be partially masked with pieces of shrubbery. For reed warblers the trap should be placed among reeds at the edge of a water pool.

When recommending cage traps for birds it is worth remembering that these need not necessarily be ones especially designed for them. Some of the mammal traps which have been described can be quite adequate and if one of these is already owned it might as well be given a trial. Of course most of them are single-catch traps, and the size of the trap, especially with regard to the delicacy of the setting mechanism, must be appropriate for the birds to be caught. Birds are very much lighter in weight than mammals of comparable size and their legs and feet are often quite slender, so a mammal trap would have to be set very finely in order to catch a bird. Also, mammal traps often have double automatic doors, intended to be fixed open and baited for some time with the trap mechanism out of action. This is to give shy mammals confidence in approaching a trap by being able to see straight through it. This ruse can also be used for shy birds, leaving the trap baited but not set. When the bait is regularly disappearing the trip mechanism can be set to catch.

Various forms of sparrow cage traps are available. Most of

them are multicatch with various forms of funnel entrances. The Government trap, designed and used by the Ministry of Agriculture, Fisheries and Food in Britain, has a semi-cylindrical framework measuring 4 by 2ft (1.2 by 0.6m) at the base. It is similar to a fish trap having a funnel entrance at one end in the ½in (13mm) wire-mesh covering the trap. This leads into a floorless compartment, giving the sparrow more confidence to enter. Across the middle of the trap is a wire-mesh partition which contains a second funnel leading to a second compartment, but this has a mesh floor so that the catch can be removed even when the trap is picked up.

Traps like this one and an upright cylindrical version with funnels around the base, can be adapted for catching waterfowl, especially ducks. The upright one was designed by the Frankfurt ringing station in West Germany.

Either semi-cylindrical or rectangular wire-net cages are mounted on wooden platforms under which are fastened empty petrol (gasolene) cans to act as floats. There are two alternative methods used to encourage the ducks to enter the trap. One used in a trap designed by P. A. D. Hollom has a detachable cage and initially the platform, suitably baited with soaked bread, is floated without the cage to encourage the ducks to feed on it. The Fordingbridge trap used by the Eley Game Research Station in Hampshire has sliding lids which are left off for the preliminary pre-baiting period. These floating traps are quite large, measuring 6 by 4ft (1.8 by 1.2m) at the base and have funnels which taper from 12in (305mm) on the outside to 5in (127mm) at the inner end.

While baits have been included as essentials for most forms of bird trapping, readers might like to know that other means of attracting birds have been used. Some people are able to imitate bird calls quite realistically and this can be used to draw birds towards a trap, but it is usual to find more people who think that they have this gift than those who really have developed the art to perfection. For those who recognize that the ability to imitate bird calls is not theirs, it is possible to buy various whistles which, when it is known what the natural call is like, can be used to produce bird-attracting sounds. Such whistles can produce passable imitations of wood pigeons, doves, pheasants, plovers, jays, warblers and cuckoos. Generally a separate whistle is needed for each kind of call.

There have been some effective experiments undertaken in attracting birds to traps by using recordings of bird calls. The small cassette recorders and players can be useful, as they are very easy to conceal and tapes covering a wide range of bird songs and calls are available commercially.

Live birds have been used as decoys and some cage traps have been manufactured with additional decoy pens attached to them. If the decoy is protected in a pen and not tethered or maimed in any way, such a use is permissible in Britain, always provided that there is a supply of food and water and that it is visited at least once every twenty-four hours. Tethering a bird to a trap, maiming one to prevent it from escaping, or blinding one, are all practices that have been used to attract predatorial birds, but are now illegal in Britain.

Aviary Traps

These of course are cage traps, but whereas most of those that have just been described are portable and intended, even in the multicatch types, for taking not more than fifteen to twenty birds at a time, the aviary traps are very large and can take large numbers of birds such as crows, magpies and pigeons. They may be constructed on the site where they will be used, or they could be made in sections like portable buildings and bolted together.

The main purpose of these traps is to control the numbers of bird pests in the medium-to-large-size group and while they are likely to be used mostly by farmers and fruit growers who are anxious to protect their crops, they can also be used on the flat tops of buildings in towns and cities where pigeons are a menace, or even in the vicinity of airports where flocks of birds can provide a hazard for aircraft landing or taking off. They can also be used by bird ringing stations where large numbers of birds are involved, but the trap pattern for this purpose may be at a slight variance from the box shape usually associated with aviaries.

In Britain, the Ministry of Agriculture, Fisheries and Food has led the way in designing these traps, in response to a demand from horticulturists and farmers for a means of protecting their crops from pests. Sometimes farm livestock may also require protection especially when crows attack new-born lambs.

The first of these traps to be designed, the Mark 1, is the ladder trap, so named for the reason obvious from Figure 27. The chief requirements to build this trap, which has a 12 by 9ft (3.7 by 2.7m) base and is 6ft (1.8m) high, are pieces of 2 by 2in (50 by 50mm) lumber, preferably planed smooth, and 1in (25mm) galvanized hexagonal wire-mesh, known in Britain as chicken wire. The ladder is 9in (230mm) wide and five rungs spaced 3in (75mm) apart are built from each end. In the centre of the ladder the rungs are spaced at intervals of 9in (230mm). There is a 2ft (0.6m) wide door in one side through which captive birds can be removed. Except for the ladder, the framework is covered with wire-mesh which can be stapled in place, but first the wood should be coated with any non-toxic preservative.

This trap can use a live decoy, such as a hen, so long as the legislation concerning such a use is observed in Britain, but it might be easier and just as efficient to use grain, such as maize, or soaked bread, as bait. Birds emboldened to enter through gaps in the ladder never seem to fly upwards to escape by the same route. It may take time before birds begin to invade the trap and they can be encouraged by placing it under tree cover where a gradual approach in apparent safety is possible by moving from one perch to another.

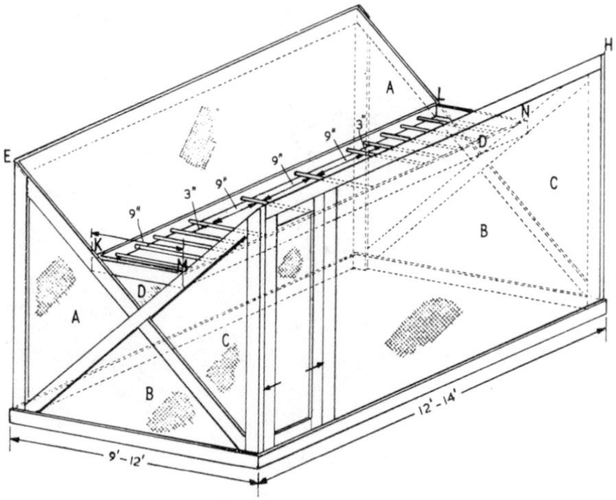

Fig 27 Ladder-type cage trap

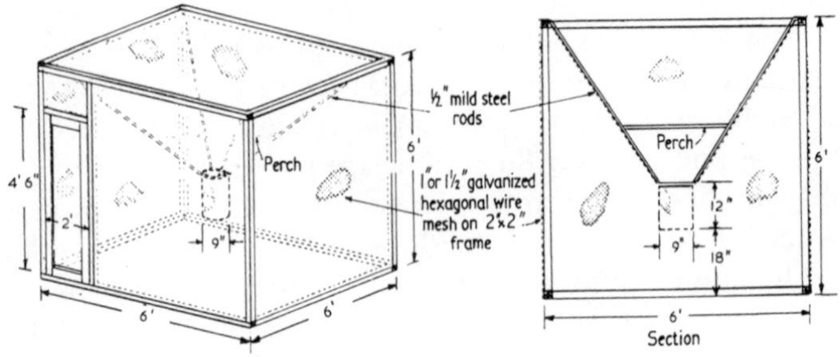

Fig 28 Funnel-type cage trap

Because the birds may be scared by an observed association between a trap and a man, it is recommended that the captive birds are removed at dusk. During daylight hours it is unlikely that a trap could be entered unseen by the countless birds likely to be occupying the surrounding vegetation.

Figure 28 shows the Mark 2 trap, which is quite obviously a funnel trap, although it can be seen that the funnel is inverted from the roof of the aviary. As with the Mark 1 trap, the basic

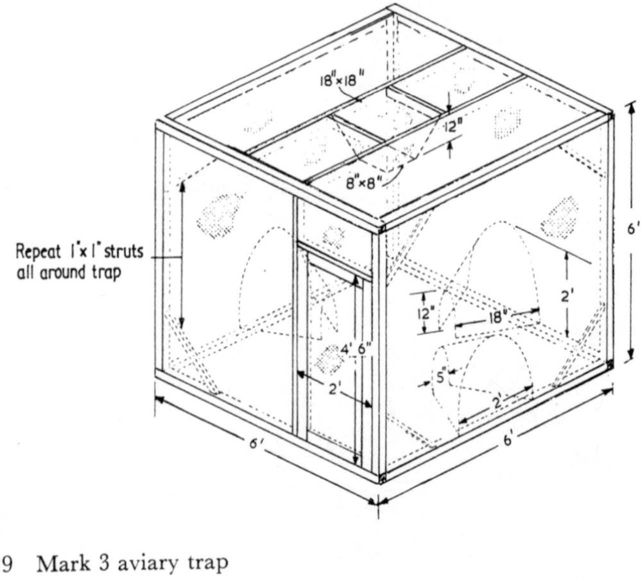

Fig 29 Mark 3 aviary trap

materials are 2 by 2in (50 by 50mm) lumber to form the 6ft (1.8m) cube framework. Again, one side has a 2ft (0.6m) wide door and the four sides are covered with 1in (25mm) wire-mesh. The funnel frame, or hopper, is constructed by bolting four ½in (13mm) mild steel rods, one to each top corner. The lower ends are spot-welded to a 9in (230mm) steel ring. The sides of the hopper are lined with 1in (25mm) wire mesh and to the ring is fastened a ¾in (20mm) wire-mesh tube reaching down for 12in (305mm) so that it ends 18in (457mm) above the ground. The siting and baiting of this trap are the same as with the Mark 1.

The Mark 3 trap has greater versatility than have the first two and by virtue of bracing placed across the corners of the framework, it is stronger. As seen in Figure 29, it owes its increased catching performance to alternative methods of entry, either through inverted funnels in the roof of the cage, or by funnels leading in from the sides of the base. Like the other two it also has a door in the side for removing the catch. Crows will usually favour entrance through the ground-level funnels, whereas jackdaws will go in through those at the top. Rooks have no preferences and will enter all the funnels equally well.

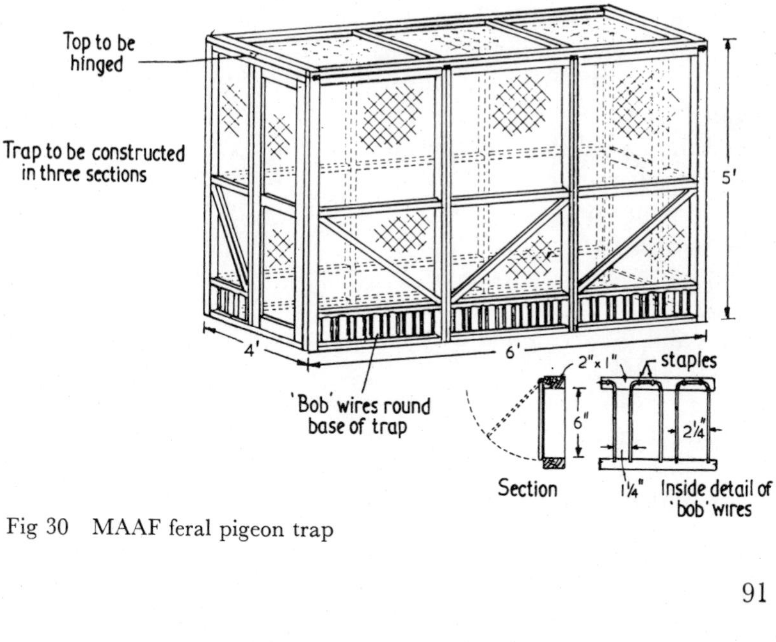

Fig 30 MAAF feral pigeon trap

The final trap designed for corvids is the Mark 4. It is bigger than Marks 2 and 3, being 12 by 6ft (3.7 by 1.8m) at the base and is simpler in construction through having only 4in (100mm) rope sheep-netting fastened over the top. While this is fastened taut at the beginning, it soon sags to form a cone through which birds will enter. It can be baited like the others, but consideration might be given to using the carcase of a dead sheep, a rabbit or a hare if the purpose is to catch crows.

The MAAF trap for feral pigeons is seen in Figure 30. Its measurements are 6 by 4ft (1.8 by 1.2m) at the base and it has a height of 5ft (1.5m). Because it may often be used on the flat tops of buildings where pigeons congregate, it needs to be made in sections so that it can be carried through the doors of offices and other rooms as well as into lifts to take it to the roof. The framework is made from 2 by 2in (50 by 50mm) lumber and is covered with 1in (25mm) galvanized wire mesh, except for the 6in (152mm) high area immediately above the baseline. In this area inverted U-shaped bob wires are fastened. They are suspended from the top frame of the gap by means of staples. They can be pushed inwards by birds but the bottoms of the legs of the wires push up against the bottom of the frame if the birds try to push out again. The bob wires are made of 10 swg welding wire or some similar material. Doors 2ft (0.6m) wide are built into each end of the aviary.

In urban areas flat rooftops form the best sites for these traps to avoid the interference likely if they were placed on the ground. None the less, they should be sited where pigeons are proving to be a nuisance, but because of the traffic noise down below there are large numbers of pigeons on building tops. In the rural areas, where disturbance is less likely, the pigeons will have no fear of dropping to the ground and pushing through the bob wires to get at the bait inside. The best form of bait is a mixture of wheat, maize and New Zealand maple peas, all soaked and in a weight ratio of 1:2:4.

Pigeons can be encouraged to enter the trap by leaving the top section off and having the doors open at each end for a few days. When they are used to the trap, the top and the doors can be closed. Small wooden boxes can be placed inside to give cover and water should be available. Occasionally, in areas where pigeon

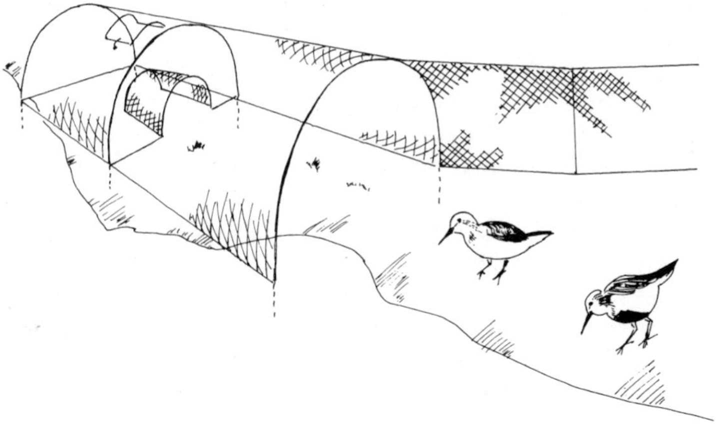

Fig 31 Dunlin trap

fanciers are to be found, a homing racing pigeon may get into the trap. They usually have a coded ring on one of the their legs and a local member of the fancy will be able to read this and arrange to have the bird returned to its owner.

A trap to catch dunlin on the island of Skokholm off the south-west coast of Wales, could also be used for other waders. It is seen in Figure 31 as a tapering funnel not unlike an abbreviated pipe of a duck decoy. The trap is about 6ft (1.8m) in length and at the mouth end it is 2ft 6 in (0.8m) wide at the base and 2ft (0.6m) high. It tapers to a height of 9in (230mm) at the rear end, but 18in (457mm) from the end there is a partition which makes a compartment entered by birds pushing through a small secondary funnel at the bottom of the partition. The top of the end compartment, or coop, has a hatch door. The trap is constructed from hoops of strong galvanized iron rod over which is stretched fine ½in (13mm) wire-mesh. The hoops have points filed on their ends and these extend beyond the mesh so that the traps can be pinned into the mudbanks where they are sited. It is an improvement to provide a guide wall extending for several feet from one side of the trap mouth. The method of operating the trap is not unlike that used in a decoy pipe. The waders are 'walked' by a ringer into the outer funnel in the way that a decoyman or dog would do with a decoy pipe, and once inside this they are flushed into the inner section. Removal is through the hatch in the roof of the coop.

The Heligoland trap, which gets its name from a prototype used at a bird observatory site on the Heligoland Bight, is in some respects like a giant dunlin trap and is even more like a wildfowl decoy in size, although it does not have a stream of water running through the net.

These traps are now operated at most coastal bird observatories, being placed beside sand dunes or hedges, even among shrubs, to give a semblance of natural conditions. Their size is such that small trees can be planted inside to give some masking of the artificiality. The entrance (see Figure 32) may be 40 or 50ft (12 or 15m) wide and 10ft (3m) high, but more usually will be about half of this width and about 8ft (2.4m) high. The entrance usually has wing nets of 1in (25mm) wire-mesh which guide or funnel the birds towards it, also a perching wire 18in (457mm) below the roof for flycatchers. From the entrance the trap angles sharply away for about 20ft (6m) and at this stage is covered with ⅝in

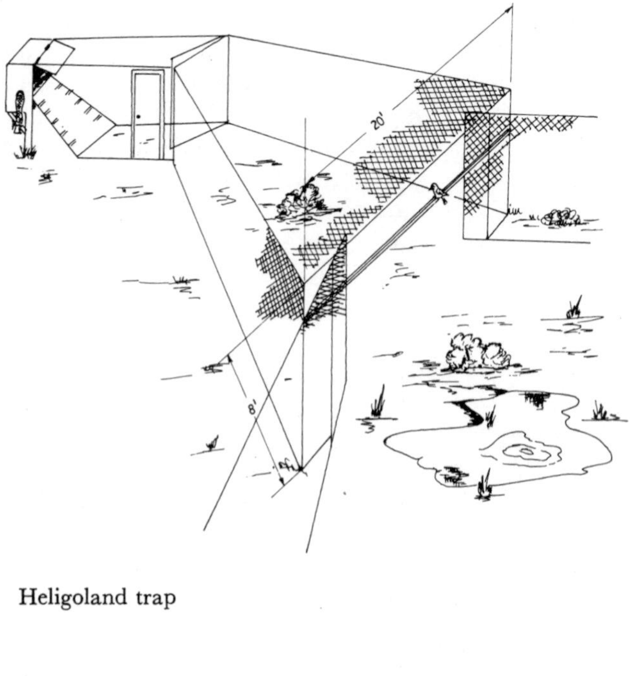

Fig 32 Heligoland trap

(15mm) wire-mesh netting before angling back again until the width is reduced to 3½ft (1m). Between these two sections there is a swing door operated from the entrance area by a cord. In the final section, which is of ½in (13mm) mesh, the floor slopes upward towards a collecting box seen in the enlarged drawing. It is at a height of about 6ft (1.8m).

Using artificial or natural cover, a ringer (bander) will flush birds into the trap urging them beyond the swing door which is then closed. Once inside the collecting box the lid is released by a remotely controlled cord. The back of the box is glazed with two sheets of glass the uppermost of which slopes downwards and the lower one is vertical. After striking the upper sheet of glass the fluttering birds slide down to drop through a gap in a platform extending two-thirds of the distance from front to back. In the sides of the lower compartment are holes with sleeves made from heavyweight nylon socks and through these the birds can be removed for ringing. The door in the last netting enclosure permits entrance without disturbing the swing door.

This kind of trap is used mainly for catching passerine birds.

Trapping with Nets

Nets for taking birds are used in either of two main ways, as clap nets or as mist nets.

The clap nets can be controlled automatically when they are small, or they can, and usually are, manually operated when they are large. The difference in size may be related to the size of the bird to be taken, although the automatic versions are more particularly suitable for single catches. The large clap nets are most frequently used to trap small flocks of birds or larger birds such as ducks and geese.

The automatic trap depends upon a coil spring which activates the clap net and it is set in motion when a bird takes bait placed in a pan, or when it enters the trap after being attracted by a decoy.

Small sparrow traps can be obtained in a form shown in Figure 33. They are constructed from a wooden baseboard measuring 30 by 20in (762 by 508mm) and about 1in (25mm) thick. Across the middle of this is fastened an 18in (457mm) coil wire spring.

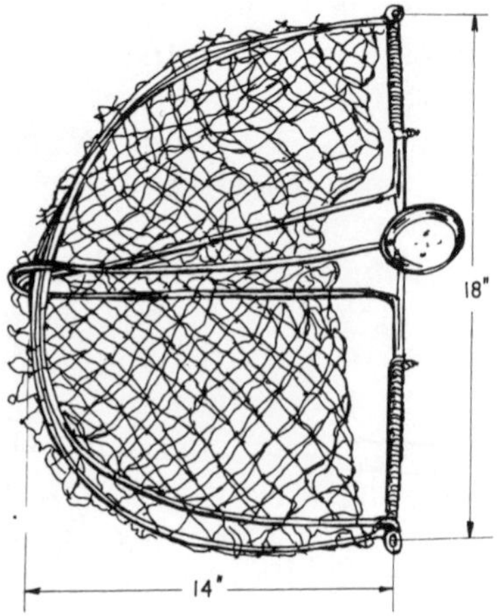

Fig 33 Sparrow net trap

The ends of the spring are extended to form a wire frame 14in (355mm) high and this is covered with a ½in (13mm) mesh stout nylon net.

On one end of the bed a 15in (380mm) long trigger is stapled to allow it to hold the net down when this is pulled back flat on the baseboard, towards the staple end. A 2½in (64mm) diameter bait pan is pivoted over the centre of the spring. The trigger end of the pan has a small hole punched into its rim and this is the catch for the trigger when the trap is set. Setting should be as fine as possible.

If the trap is to be set for sparrows, a variety of baits can be used, including almost any soaked grain such as maize, barley or wheat; also soaked bread and dried fruit such as raisins can be used.

The siting of the trap must be at any place known to be frequented by sparrows and for these birds it is not necessary to use any camouflage. For starlings, which are more timid, certainly as far as strange objects are concerned, the trap should be placed close to some kind of shrubbery or anything else which will provide cover. If the baseboard is of wood then it is a good idea to have this stained green or brown, similarly the metal parts and also the net should be stained.

Larger versions of these traps often dispense with the baseboard and instead there is a double wire frame, both parts of which are netted. Without the baseboard the trap would be too light in weight and so it would need to be fastened to the ground using metal plugs or skewers the ends of which are bent over the net frame on one side. Such traps can be used for pigeons or crows. They are less conspicuous than the wooden-based versions, especially if placed in medium to long grass, although care must be taken to ensure that the movement of the net is not impeded.

If crows are being trapped, they can be attracted using offal as a bait, or the entrails of a rabbit or a hare. For most birds of the corvid family the traps can be placed in the open.

An even stronger version of these traps is marketed in Britain by the firm of Gilbertson and Page, Ltd. They call it a 'hoodie' crow trap, as it was designed for taking hooded crows. These birds have similar habits to those of the carrion crows, but are recognized from the grey mantle and underparts and because they tend to congregate in flocks. The hoodie crow trap, which is similar to the others in action, has double springs to propel the net, stretched over a steel rod frame. The frame of the ground section of the net is drilled to take steel pegs for anchoring it to the ground.

A much more sophisticated portable and automatic net trap is one designed to capture goshawks. These birds are much favoured by falconers because they can be used satisfactorily in wooded country where they use their short tail and narrow wingspan to advantage among the trees. Goshawks tend to take their prey when it has perched, making a sudden dash for it at this stage. This is their undoing when the goshawk trap is used, because it has two main features, one of which is to use a live decoy in a cage section; the other feature is a double-frame clap-net.

The decoy cage forms the base and is cylindrical in form with both a perch for the decoy and pans for its food and water. Above the decoy cage (see illustration on page 67) the trap nets are arranged so that half is vertical and, by means of a lever on one side, the other half is extended horizontally. The trap is particularly novel because when the hawk dives on the decoy, it lands on the horizontal net, which quickly claps shut against the vertical half, imprisoning the hawk. At the same time the door in the decoy cage springs open and the bird inside, usually a dove, is able to escape. In principle the use of the trap is combined with that of a dovecote placed nearby, so that the escaping dove can immediately home to it.

The British and European goshawk is *Accipiter gentilis gentilis*, but in North America there is a different one, *A. g. atricapillis*. Both are birds which favour wooded country at a range of altitudes.

While these small net traps work on the clap-net principle, the name clap-net is usually reserved for the large manually operated types. These are the traps often used by ringers (banders) for taking small wading birds when they are in flocks, or even birds as large as ducks and geese. The nets can be set up on mudbanks in a river estuary or alongside lakes in situations where migrant forms land to feed.

Clap-nets can be double structures with two nets working simultaneously, but these tend to be cumbersome and nowadays most ornithologists prefer the portable and better controlled single-net variety. The clap-net seen in Figure 34 would be hand-operated and any size between 9 by 4ft (2.7 by 1.2m) and 15 by by 6ft (4.6 by 1.8m) but there are extremely large versions measuring 60 by 20ft (18 by 6m) which can be used for catching

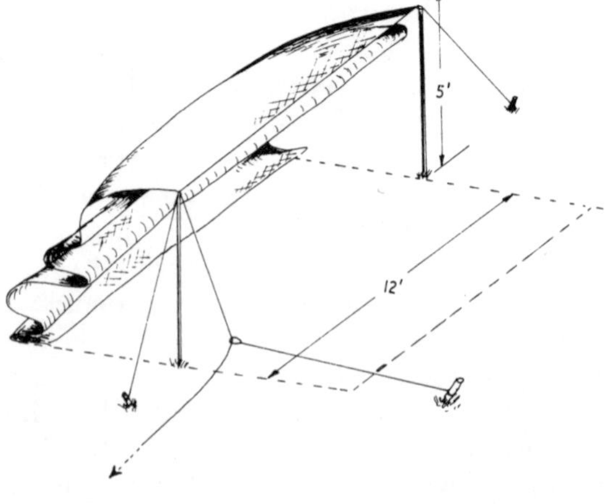

Fig 34 Clap net

geese, although they are too big to be operated unaided by a single person and have a spring-loaded mechanism to assist the man-triggered draw-cord.

A simple version can easily be made from two poles, each of which should be half of the width of the fully extended net. They should be light in weight and have a hole drilled a short way from one end. Through these holes a short greased-leather thong should be threaded and in each case the thong is tied around the eyelet end of a metal skewer or tent peg to make a hinged base for each pole. Between pegs, some distance on each side of the poles, is stretched a guy rope which goes through eyelets at the tops of the pegs and so secures the edge of the net; so the poles must be the width of the net apart. The rear edge of the net is pegged into a trench dug at a distance of half of its length from the poles and the soil, sand or mud that is dug out is afterwards replaced to seal the edge of the net.

The drawcord must be long enough to reach an operator who is concealed at some distance from the net. It passes through a brass ring tied to a shorter cord which in turn is tied to a peg at some distance along the line where the net will fall. A tension is created when the drawcord is pulled and this produces a rapid action which closes the net.

When the net is collapsed there is a flat and unimpeded area which will hold out no apparent signs of danger for birds and if a suitable bait is provided they will be positively encouraged to move into the trapping zone. Remembering that these traps are not intended for other than wading birds, suitable baits could include a concentrated supply of any of the natural foods they look for in muddy shores, especially molluscs and various worms. These would have to be dug out in advance and scattered within the trap area, but the operator would have to be ready for action because most of these small shore-living creatures can burrow very rapidly and would therefore escape. It would also pay to study the feeding habits of the birds to be trapped, particularly the times when they are on the shores, often on an ebbing tide in estuaries, but especially during the early morning and evening alongside the shores of a river or lake.

The last of the net traps to be described is that which has gained increasing prominence among bird ringers in recent years, but has also been used to catch songbirds and birds for the dining table in many countries where the legislation does not require any form of licensing. This is the mist net which was developed by the Japanese and first used in Britain in the 1950s. Now more than half of the birds ringed each year in the British Isles are mist-netted.

Fig 35 Mist net with pockets over shelf strings

The original Japanese nets were made of fine silken threads, but those used now are of nylon or Terylene fibres which, when dyed black, are virtually invisible to birds. A net is set up as shown in Figure 35 so that tight shelf strings are stretched horizontally at intervals between two poles. The shelf strings are threaded through the mesh of the net, which may be as much as 60ft (18m) long and 9ft (2.7m) high. The mesh is usually $1\frac{1}{4}$ to $1\frac{1}{2}$in (32 to 38mm) and when birds fly against it their momentum carries the net over a shelf string below and it forms a pocket into which they drop. While, strictly, the birds are not caught in the mesh but in the pocket, they do in fact get slightly entangled and ringers must be on hand to release them as soon as possible. This demands a great deal of skill on the part of the operator because it is not uncommon for up to 200 birds to be caught in the net at one time. For this reason the use of mist nets in Britain is restricted to persons who have had a thorough training in handling them.

The nets can be used in a wide range of situations, but woodland areas are very suitable because the nets are so much less noticeable in them. Gardens with shrubberies or well-cultivated

Duffus mole trap

An Arouze cage trap

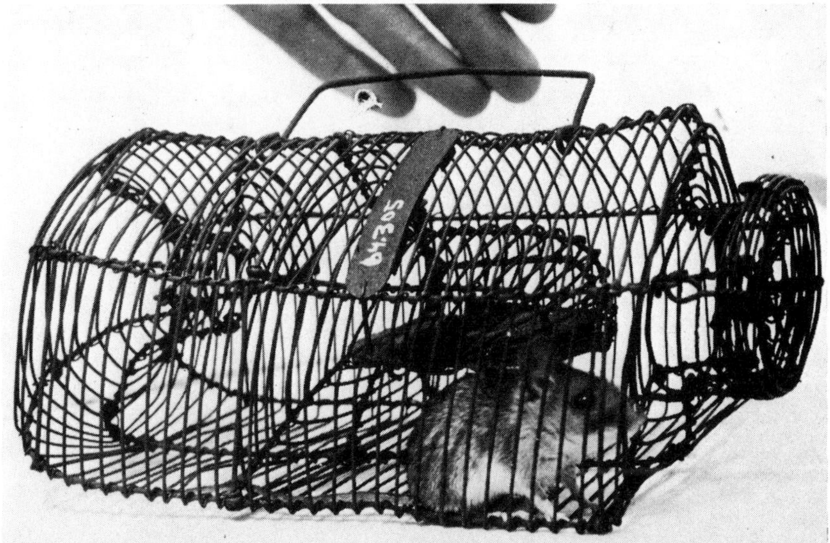

The Martin cage trap

Whole family rat trap

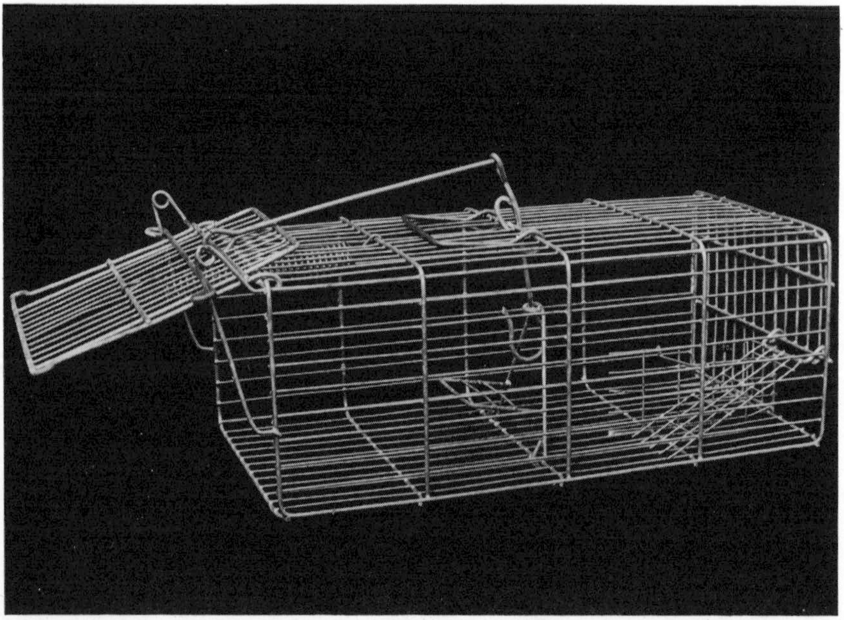

herbaceous borders can be excellent trapping places. These nets can also be used for catching waders when stretched across an estuarine or lakeside shore, because such birds frequently rise in small flocks at the edge of the water, moving on a short distance before settling to resume feeding.

Having mentioned that mist nets can be used near to the edge of water, a caution is necessary because it is essential that the nets do not get wet: if they do they would not form loose pockets when birds struck them, instead the netting sides of the pockets would adhere to each other and the birds would be severely entangled. Similarly, the nets cannot be used in windy conditions because of the difficulty in forming pockets and, should they be formed, of birds being subjected to blowing about in the net. It must be made clear that mist nets are of no use when birds are not flying about.

Legislation

In Britain, the Protection of Birds Acts 1954–67 apply. The full details of these are too extensive to be included here. The Act can be obtained from HMSO bookshops, or a summary of the provisions is given in a small booklet sold by the Royal Society for the Protection of Birds (RSPB).

British bird protection lists birds in categories. For example, Part 1 of the First Schedule includes birds and their eggs protected by special penalties at all times. Part 2 of this schedule includes birds and eggs protected by special penalties during a close season between 1 February and 31 August. The list includes whimbrel and a number of species of wild duck (except that over areas below high water mark the start of the close season is delayed until 21 February for duck).

The Second Schedule includes birds usually regarded as pests by farmers, fruit growers and horticulturists as well as owners of fish hatcheries. These birds may be killed by persons in the approved categories, although for some birds this applies only in certain specified areas—for example, bullfinches in fruit-growing counties only.

The Third Schedule includes waterfowl and gamebirds which may be taken or killed outside a close season which generally occurs between 1 February and 31 August, but most eggs are protected at all times.

The Fourth Schedule covers the birds which may not be sold alive unless close-ringed and bred in captivity.

There are some important details for would-be bird trappers. Ringing is only permitted by persons who have obtained a licence issued by the Natural Environment Research Council (NERC). Under this licence only officially numbered rings issued by the British Trust for Ornithology (BTO) can be used and a BTO permit necessary to get these will only be given to a person fully trained by a licensed ringer. It is illegal to colour-ring birds without a NERC licence.

A licence is required before birds of prey can be taken for use in falconry and a second licence is required to kill wild birds in the course of falconry.

Various licences are available for taking, killing or injuring birds for scientific experimental purposes under the Cruelty to Animals Act 1976. Licences are also available for selling or importing birds for scientific and educational purposes and these will specify the number and species of the birds involved, the areas from which they may be taken and the methods for taking them.

With particular reference to birds in Britain, pole traps, that is, steel or spring traps fastened to the tops of poles, intended especially for taking birds of prey as a means for protecting game birds, are illegal. They are rightly considered inhumane because any bird, not just a predator, could be caught by the feet when alighting on the pole. They then hang by the feet to die a lingering and obviously painful death. The RSPB has been vigilant in bringing the illegal uses of these traps to notice and their users to justice. Similarly, the use of bird lime on twigs and branches of trees for catching birds is illegal in Britain.

On the European mainland there is either an indifference to bird protection and a consequent lack of legislation or, as in the case of Belgium, a fluctuating situation. In Italy Federal legislation was enacted in 1971 to ban the shooting of spring migrants. In 1972 when new regional governments came into force, the provinces of Campagna, Calabria and Apulia passed laws to allow spring shooting.

In the United States there is variable legislation concerning bird protection and the use of traps for catching birds. As with other aspects of wildlife protection this is, as in Italy, largely the result of the Federal Government handing over the responsibility for wildlife control to individual states. In Wisconsin pole traps have been prohibited, largely the result of an educational campaign by the North Eastern Wisconsin Audubon Society. It is acknowledged that throughout the United States pole trapping has always been a secretive activity, but set around trout rearing ponds, the estates of hunting clubs and gamebird farms, these traps have taken a heavy toll of herons, kingfishers, owls and hawks.

In Canada the Canadian Wildlife Service administers a Migratory Birds Convention Act, which aims to control the hunting of migratory birds by the operation of close seasons which vary from one province to another. Reference should be made to the Act for details, but additional control is exercised by issuing permits, limiting the bag size and regulating the sale and shipment of birds, skins or eggs taken with a permit during an open season. While the Act concentrates upon hunting by shooting, the interpretation of the terms used in the Act specifically associates trapping with the term 'hunt'.

3 Trapping Fish

The term 'fish' is not used here in the strict zoological sense. In the commercial world, and for the layman, 'fish' includes creatures such as crabs, lobsters, prawns, shrimps and crayfish, also the various kinds of edible molluscs, such as mussels, cockles, winkles and oysters.

Traps have been devised to capture all of these aquatic animals. Line fishing or the use of nets, when they are trailed or hauled, are not sedentary methods and are not covered here.

Pot Traps

Throughout the world there is a long history of fish-trapping with what are commonly called 'pots' or 'creels' for taking crabs, lobsters and other similar crustaceans.

The basic structure is a box-like container found in various shapes and sizes and made from all manner of materials. Traditionally pots have been made like baskets from wickerwork or from wooden laths. Sometimes a wooden framework has been covered with netting. More recently metal pots have been used; often, because they may have to resist the effects of seawater, they are protected from corrosion by plastic coatings or have other anticorrosive treatments. In an age when a multitude of synthetic plastic resins are available for constructional purposes, it is not surprising to find plastic pots being made, in some cases by conversion from objects never originally intended as traps.

Whatever the material used or the shape produced, the pots work on the same principle: they have to be weighted in order to take them down to the sea bottom—not a great distance, since they are mostly used inshore or in estuaries—because the lobsters and similar creatures tend to be bottom-living. Somewhere in the pot, often at the top but sometimes at the sides, there will be one or more openings through which the animals can crawl. To provide for the essentials of a trap the openings lead inside through funnels, which become progressively more narrow. The animals will push their way through because inside the pot there is some kind of bait, often pieces of fish tied to the bottom. While they can push into the pot, they find it impossible to push out again because the funnels, which are usually made of net, go slack and offer no resistance to the thrust. These pots are therefore live-traps and the captives are certain to be fresh when the pots are hauled in.

The crab and lobster fishermen who use these pots go out from the shores in small craft heavily laden with the gear. The pots are usually planted in clusters at favourite spots known to the men, although on a non-commercial basis some amateurs catch with one or two pots just to supply their own needs.

Each pot has a stone or brick, even a lump of iron, to provide enough weight to sink it, also a length of rope to stretch between the bottom and the surface where it is fastened to a float. The float may be a sophisticated buoy which has been purpose-made or, in its simplest form, a block of wood. The float or buoy will often carry a marker in the form of a pennant, and in an area where several fishermen are sowing pots the colours of the pennants identify the owners of the pots beneath.

The pots are left for intervals of twenty-four hours between hauls after which they must be re-baited and dropped again if the area is productive; otherwise they are stored aboard the boat and moved elsewhere. The captives are removed through a trap door and in the case of crabs and lobsters a certain knack is necessary to avoid being nipped by the powerful claws. Crabs are grasped from behind with the thumb on the upper shell and the fingers on the body below. Lobsters are grasped around the body behind the front pair of large clawed limbs. They are taken ashore alive and put into boiling water which simultaneously kills and cooks them, turning their colour from the natural blue-green to the familiar pinky-red seen when they are brought to the table.

With crab and lobster fishing there is always a certain element of luck, but local expertise in knowing likely spots to drop the pots, bearing in mind the season and the tidal conditions, will play an important part. There is often competition among local fishermen in getting to the best places; alternatively there may be a private arrangement between them to allocate or zone the areas. It is always a good idea for a newcomer to an established fishing area to get to know the local situation rather than to take matters into his own hands. In any case it is likely to take time to achieve acceptance by a local community, if at all. 'Foreigners' have sometimes created a feud which has lasted through several generations of families.

In many areas lobster fishing is controlled by some kind of legislation; almost certainly this limits the size of the lobsters which can be taken and experienced lobstermen use pots with spaces in the framework or mesh which allow 'off-limits' sizes to escape. It is also usual to return female lobsters and crabs which are in 'berry'—that is to say, those carrying their eggs conveniently exposed on the outside of their bodies. Licences are needed in some areas for lobsters; for example, in the United States, in the state of Maine, a licence will allow fishing in any of the state waters and the same state also registers the colour codes used on the buoys. Around Maine, fishing can go on throughout the year, but nearby Canadian control is much tighter, so that

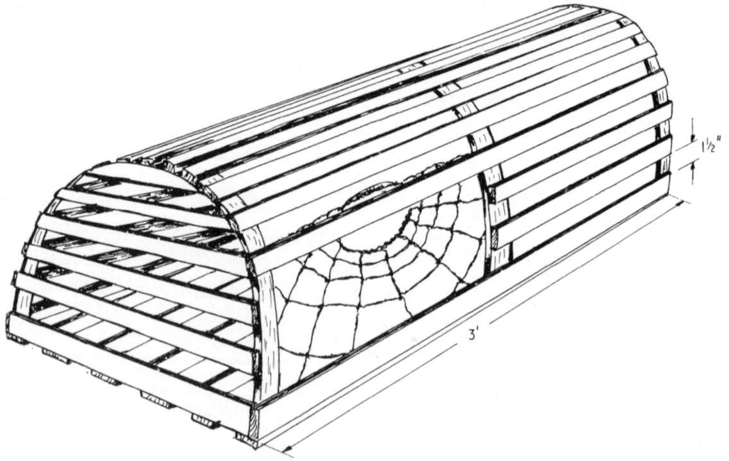

Fig 36 Traditional American lobster pot

off Prince Edward Island fishing can only take place during the summer months on the south shore. In Britain under the Immature Crabs and Lobsters Order 1976, the minimum size for crabs of the species *Cancer pagurus* is 4in (115mm) across the broadest part of the back, and for lobsters a carapace of 3in (80mm) measured from the rear of the eye socket to the rear of the shell, along a line parallel to the mid-line of the body shell.

Some Pot Designs

The almost universal American pot, the one which is hand-made during the winter months or the closed season, is a half cylinder. It is some 3ft (0.9m) long and consists of a framework, often of oak with slats or lars of spruce. The slats are spaced 1½in (38mm) apart, the distance which allows the undersized lobsters to escape. The openings at one end have a funnel-shaped net which nowadays is made of nylon. The pot is attached to a warp line at the other end of which is the coloured buoy, formerly of wood but now usually of styroform. An example is seen in Figure 36.

A variation of this half-cylinder pattern is a rectangular box shape, but in both styles stones are used as weights in the bottom and pieces of fresh or salted fish are used as bait. The bait is now often obtained from nearby fish processing plants.

Such traps have been used in the United States and Canada for more than a hundred years, but while they are effective, they can hardly be considered durable and many new forms have been tried, some, as far as durability goes, being particularly successful. One example is a plastic-covered steel lobster pot of quite large proportions when compared with conventional traps. It was developed by the Bureau of Commercial Fisheries at Gloucester, Massachusetts and measures 5 by 4 by 2ft (1.5 by 1.2 by 0.6m). Despite a weight of 138lb (62.6kg) it is recommended for lifting every twenty-four hours with a catch that can regularly weigh 10lb (4.5kg) and even as much as 20lb. Compared with a regular catch averaging ½lb (0.2kg) from traditional traps, these new traps obviously make economic sense, once they and a boat big enough to carry them have been paid for.

In Britain and on the Continent all manner of pots are used, but one of the most common is identical in size and shape to the American half-cylinder version, except that the covering of the framework is of netting, the mesh of which is gauged to allow the illegal sizes to escape.

The original pot handed down as a pattern over hundreds of years and one which has still not entirely disappeared, is the inkwell trap made of withies forming a dome over a circular base and with a wicker funnel inverted from the top of the dome (see Figure 37). They were common in the south west of England but nowadays barrel traps similar to the ones used in Scandinavia are favoured.

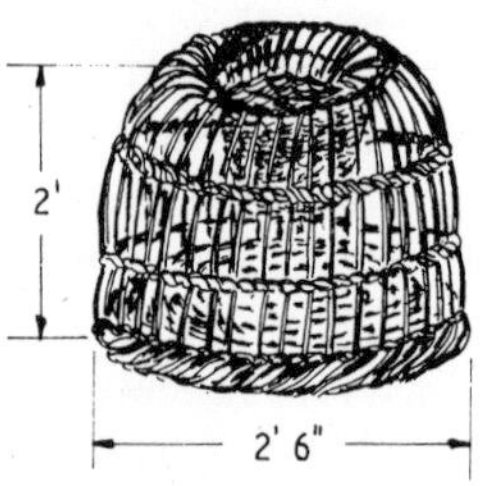

Fig 37 Inkwell trap

One instance of the way in which other objects are adapted as pots comes from Wells-next-the-sea in Norfolk, England, where large moulded plastic plant pots, about 18in (457mm) across the top, have a hole cut in the bottom from which a nylon-net funnel is suspended inside the pot. Across the open end of the pot, which in practice becomes the bottom of the trap, metal rods are threaded through holes pierced in the sides of the pot, just below the rim, to reinforce the concrete which is poured in to provide a weight for the bottom. The overall effect is of a plastic inkwell trap.

To provide for portability and also to allow more pots to be carried in a boat, a number of folding versions have been developed. A large one is the American Leakey Folding Creel seen in Figure 38, but despite its portability, it has not been as successful in withstanding heavy seas as the parlour type of trap.

The Allcock Manufacturing Company at Ossining, New York, makes traps under the Havahart brand name and one of its products is the Star Crab Trap. It is portable and consists of a square base of galvanized steel-mesh from which are hinged four triangular mesh sides. The sides are connected to a line system

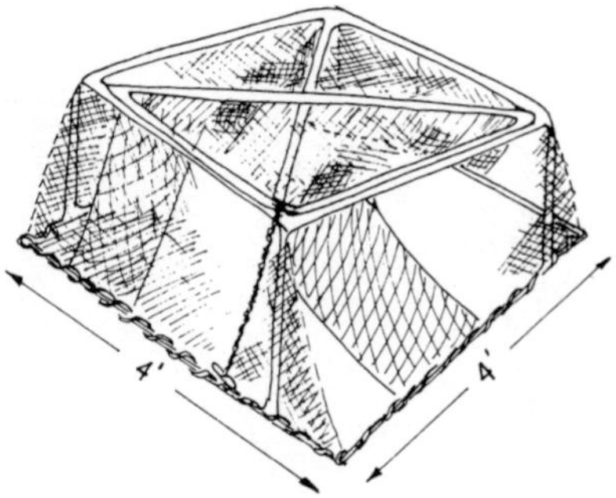

Fig 38 American Leakey folding creel

which has an open/close control. When closed the sides are pulled above the base to form a pyramid and the trap is lowered to the sea floor in this form with bait fastened to the base. When it reaches the sea bed the control is released and the sides fall out from the base to give a star-shaped pattern. The operator in the boat waits until tugging on the bait can be felt, then the rope mechanism is used to draw the sides up and so capture the crab in the pyramid. The trap is then hauled up. (See page 49.)

Net Traps

The nets about which this section is concerned are usually manufactured from netting twine, or these days from nylon yarn, but there are some small ones which are made from wire-mesh netting.

Where nets are used to catch fish, it is for the migratory forms, such as salmon or eels, and these have seasonal migrations involving journeys to and from the sea and the rivers. Traps may also be used along a shore when fish obey seasonal urges to come in from deep water, usually for breeding purposes.

The significance of using nets as traps is to provide a lure to fish that are moving on a set course in response to some behavioural life pattern, particularly associated with breeding cycles. Fixed nets, which are what make them traps, would be of little use in catching deep-sea fish, and particularly those which do not seem to possess a set movement pattern. They can, of course, stand a good chance of catching non-migratory river and

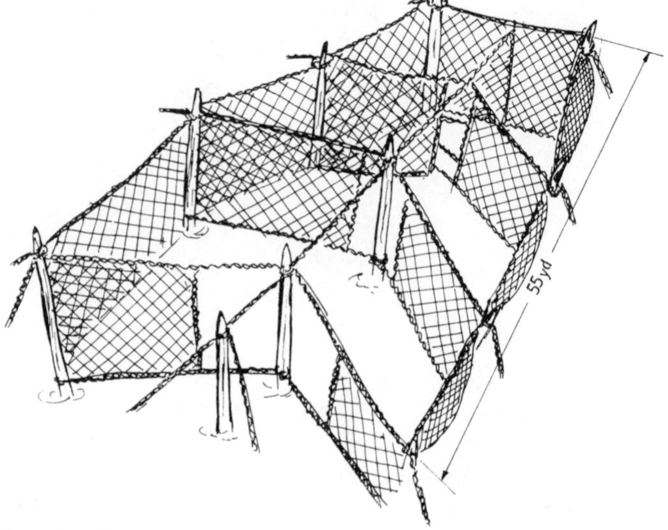

Fig 39a A staked net trap

lake fish such as trout, pike, perch and even minnows.

Salmon start their lives in rivers, but within a year, or two at the most, of hatching from eggs young salmon leave the rivers and head out to sea where they spend several years feeding, fattening and maturing. When they are ready to spawn they ascend the rivers and at this time the mass movement of these fish is known as the 'salmon run'.

With eels the reverse situation occurs. There seem to be a number of deep-sea spawning grounds throughout the world for temperate eels, including the Sargasso Sea and the Pacific Ocean north east of Australasia and also south east of Japan. The larvae which hatch from the eggs at these breeding areas would appear to migrate back to the rivers in distant countries from which the adults originally started. The time to trap eels is at the adult stage as they are leaving the rivers.

The times when salmon migrate up river vary and the legislation which fixes the open and closed seasons for trapping varies accordingly. Thus in Britain, Western Europe and Eastern Canada the salmon run associated with the Atlantic salmon takes place between March and June, whereas the various

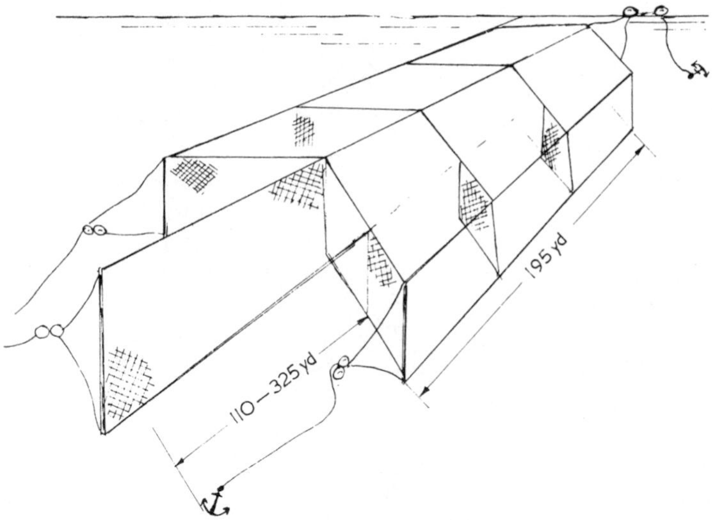

Fig 39b A floating net trap

species of the Pacific salmon, which move into the west-flowing rivers of the United States and the east-flowing Japanese rivers, migrate mainly in spring, although with the dog salmon it is in the autumn.

The use of trap nets in Scotland for catching salmon may be taken as fairly typical of the methods employed, although it should be made clear that in countries where the legislation allows—for example, Eire—weir traps may be an alternative method. There are two types of traps used in Scotland, those which are driven into the beaches and those which are anchored a short distance off shore.

While the general pattern of the net is the same for the two systems, a major difference is that the staked net has no floor as the beach serves this purpose. It follows that a floating net will need a floor to prevent captured fish from escaping. In both cases there is a quantity of supporting rope, but a further difference is the presence of cleats for attaching a net to staking poles as opposed to floats used for supporting an anchored trap (see Figures 39a and 39b). The traps are alike in having a long leader net, perhaps up to 325yd (300m), to divert fish towards the traps.

When attached to a stake net, the leader is usually tapered to correspond with the shelving shore. It will also have a mesh size small enough to prevent the salmon from 'gilling', which happens when a fish is able to push its head into a mesh, but gets caught by the gills.

An in-swimming salmon will reach the trap and be diverted still further into it by spurs which act like a funnel. Beyond these are two compartments, each of which is entered through a non-return valve, followed by a final section, the fish court or bag, entry to which is through a 'door', so staked or pegged to prevent stretching (see Figure 40). The mesh size decreases as the fish move through the trap sections.

A staked net can be carried to the beach by means of a tractor and then fastened over the stakes at low tide, but an anchored trap will have to be taken out in a boat. Of course, after the catch an anchored trap net will have to be hauled back into the boat for emptying.

Fish traps of these kinds are naturally vulnerable to tidal and climatic extremes and the owners must be aware of signs of deteriorating conditions which could result in damage and financial loss. Taking in nets, especially those anchored off-shore, can be a hazardous operation and will need to be done by sea-going fishermen who are tough and fearless.

Eels are trapped when they make their way down river as the so-called 'silver eels' on their way to the breeding grounds across the oceans. In Western Europe this occurs in the autumn and all

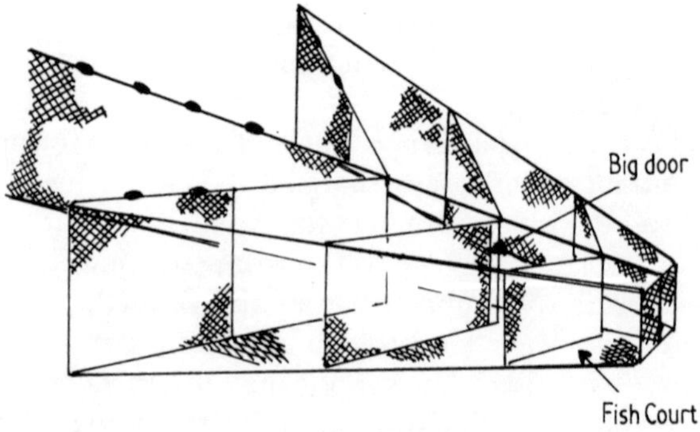

Fig 40 The fish court with its door

kinds of traps can be used. In the west-flowing River Severn net traps some 50ft (15m) in length are used. They are funnel-shaped and have a terminal trap or 'cod' which is entered through a non-return valve. The traps must be so placed that the open end faces up-stream to catch the down-swimming eels.

Elsewhere eels may be trapped using wicker baskets, also conical in shape with a wide mouth which is bell-shaped. From the mouth a basketwork funnel leads into the body of the trap and once they are inside this the eels have reached the point of no return. Although this is a primitive pattern for a fish trap, it is still effective, reasonably portable and quite durable in river estuaries. It is doubtful if these traps are sold anywhere today, although anyone keen to acquire one could probably have one made by a basket-maker.

The small portable fish traps which are obtainable from trap suppliers are those made from wire-mesh. The so-called Suffolk trap is an example. This is made of galvanized wire-mesh, is oval in cross-section and is about 3ft (0.9m) long. There is a wire-mesh funnel leading in from one end and a second funnel leads into a trap chamber one-third of the distance from the trap entrance. Fish are released from this rear chamber through a door in the end opposite that with the first funnel. This kind of trap can be used equally well for catching eels or trout, especially if baited with molluscs such as freshwater mussels. In both instances it will catch well if settled on the bottom of slow-moving river pools or shallow lakes. The trap can be lightly weighted to prevent it from drifting. If these traps are to be used in turbulent rivers they will have to be more securely anchored, by a heavy stone attached to the bottom of the trap by a length of rope. Since they will function best in fast-flowing water when they are at a mid-depth position, a further piece of rope should be connected from the top of the trap to a buoy made from an old oil drum.

In slow-running rivers, or in lakes, it can be an advantage to have a two-way trap. This is very like the Suffolk but may well be barrel-shaped and have funnels at both ends (see page 49).

Apart from shellfish there are other kinds of bait, such as pieces of liver, herring or earthworms, that can be used and they are best held in the trap by enclosing them in a can which has had holes punched in it, or in a muslin bag.

The positioning of fish traps in lakes and rivers should vary from one season to another. They can be placed in the shallows, among reeds and weeds during the summer, but in the cooler months of winter they must be much deeper so that they will be in the areas to which fish move, away from the cold surface waters.

It is still the fashion to use batteries of traps in some areas. The traps, or 'fixed engines', known in the River Severn region of England and Wales as *putchers*, are fashioned from basketwork using withies or, more recently, plastic-covered wire. They are about 6ft (1.8m) in length and 5ft (1.5m) in diameter. They are conical with a bell-shaped mouth called the *kype* which leads to a central region, the *butt*, with its valve of split withies or plastic-coated wire. Behind this and fed by another valve is the *forewheel* which is closed by means of a wooden plug. The putchers are fastened to a framework of poles driven into the mud of a river estuary, so that there are three or four rows of traps one above the other. They are meant to catch salmon, and face down-stream to take the up-swimming fish. By having the rows one above the other they will trap fish swimming at various depths at high water in a tidal river (see illustration on page 50).

Similar traps called *putts* are also used in much the same way, but are placed in pairs rather than in batteries. They have a finer valve leading from the butt to the forewheel, the purpose of this being to catch salmon in the butt and shrimps or prawns in the forewheel, which can be detached, the plug removed and the catch poured out. The wickerwork in putts is much more tightly woven than in putchers.

Legislation

Fishing of any kind is subject to legislation in and around Britain. While the purchase of a licence permits fishing using traps or 'fixed engines', to do this in a particular area or even in a specific river system, there is still the need to ensure that permission is available from the owner of the water. Laws tend to regulate the dates between which trapping can be carried out and these will vary from one region to another. Where the permission of an owner may be necessary before trapping can be undertaken in a particular patch of water, it should not be taken for granted that this will be given free of charge. There is often a rental and owners may lease long-term fishing rights to individuals or organizations such as angling clubs, so it may not always be possible to hire a stretch of water on a casual basis.

In Scotland all salmon and sea-trout fisheries are privately owned and rights are passed on from one generation of a family to the next. This also applies to the limits of territorial waters around the coastline. The administration of salmon fishing in Scotland is controlled by District Boards which enforce the Scottish Salmon Laws. These, reinforced by the Salmon Fisheries (Scotland) Protection Act 1953, are concerned with salmon conservation, limiting the size of fish taken, the season when trapping is allowed, the kinds of traps used and the mesh size of the nets. The dates of the seasons vary slightly from one locality to another, so that it is important to check the local regulations with the appropriate board. The laws also enforce the lifting of traps at the end of a season.

The laws involved are covered by the Tweed Acts of 1857 and 1859, the Tay Act of 1858 and Rivers North of the Tweed (except the Tay) Acts of 1862 and 1868. These century-old laws have been criticized recently because of a lack of legislation covering poaching and pollution. To rectify these omissions the 1951 Act deals with the problem of poaching and provides for a punishment by fines of up to £500, or imprisonment for up to two years. To deal with pollution the Rivers (Prevention of Pollution) Act 1961, strengthened in 1965, now prohibits the discharge of any mill or factory waste into rivers without the consent of the River Purification Authority. The additional schedule lists controlled waters previously suffering from pollution and makes provision to add other tidal water. Fines for offences can vary from £100 to £1,000 a day, with or without six months' imprisonment.

In England and Wales the Salmon and Freshwater Fisheries Act of 1923 brought together all the earlier laws and introduced some new measures. Under this legislation the close season for nets is 1 September to 1 February, although nets are only permissible in certain places. Weirs or dams for catching fish are banned and any that existed must have a fish pass of specified dimensions added. Dams built after 1923 have to include a fish ladder to a design approved by the Ministry of Agriculture,

Fisheries and Food and if an existing dam is altered this provision must be added.

Since 1963, the date of the Water Resources Act, new river authorities have existed and have taken over the responsibilities of the former river boards for fisheries, including the licensing.

In Ireland the Fisheries (Consolidation) Act 1959 is the statute for freshwater fishing. The fresh waters are privately owned but licences are issued by seventeen Boards of Conservators in Eire and three in Northern Ireland. In addition the two countries share control in the lucrative Foyle district through the Foyle Fisheries Commission.

As far as the Atlantic salmon is concerned, the Irish resource has made a remarkable recovery since the beginning of the century, mainly because of improved management and a vigorous restocking programme.

In the United States and Canada, the story is less fortunate. Many American rivers in the eastern states were once teeming with salmon and it is sad that now they are so often barren or at least only showing a small fraction of their original resource.

In Canada there are federal regulations which detail the maximum size of nets and the minimum size of mesh, also the weekly closure period of between thirty-six and forty-eight hours according to locality. Salmon weighing less than 5lb (2.26kg) must be returned.

In 1965 the US Congress passed the Anadromous Fish Act, the purpose of which is to supply funds to be met on a fifty–fifty basis by states, for restocking programmes. The first efforts went into a programme to improve the Penobscot River in Maine. No netting is permitted.

See-saw traps as used at the base of a wall

A mink trap (*M.A.A.F.*)

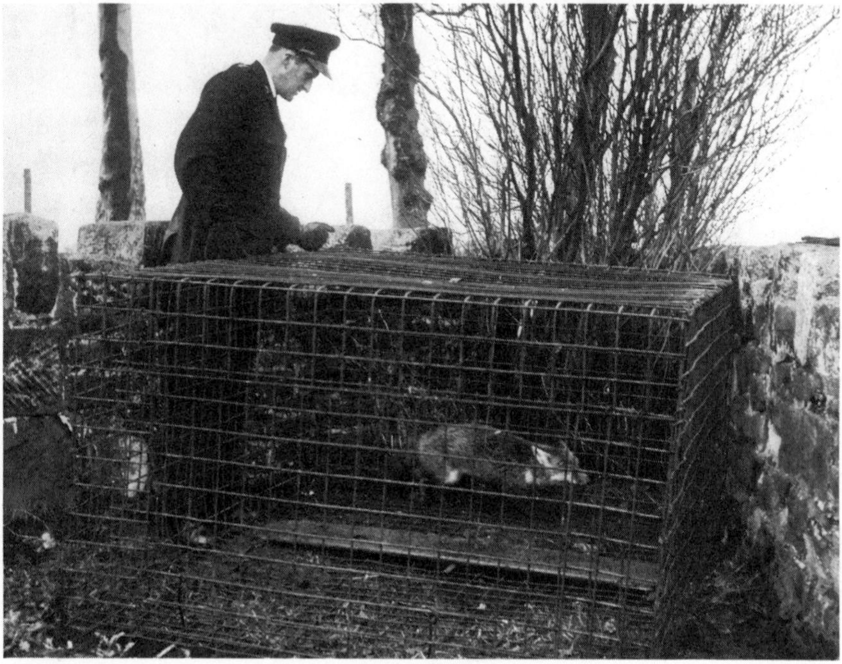

The Hunter fox trap

Havahart No 2 trap in sprung position

4 Trapping Insects

Insects were well established on earth long before the first of our own kind appeared. How our distant ancestors coped with flies, wasps and cockroaches we cannot tell, but the first chronicles of human history are full of the stories of plagues of locusts and other pestilences which wiped out crops and killed off stocks of domestic animals. To some extent we have learnt how to control insects such as the malaria-spreading mosquito and the usual garden pests. In spite of this, each growing season brings new problems for the farmer and horticulturist and we still resent being stung by wasps and bitten by fleas. It follows that anything which offers to help us to get rid of insect pests will at least get a trial and success will bring its inventor a modest fortune.

Insect traps of all kinds have been produced, many of them simple home-made affairs, others highly sophisticated and sometimes dependent for their effectiveness upon some subtle fact of science. Most, of course, are used simply to destroy pests; in a few remote parts of the world certain insects are taken as gastronomic delicacies, and the other purpose of insect trapping is for scientific research.

At its simplest as a research activity insect trapping may be a way of discovering the size and components of an insect population in a given area. Biologists are anxious to establish the extent to which different species of insects are distributed in a district, a region or a whole country. The knowledge can be useful when evaluating the interrelationships of wildlife forms—the study called ecology. When live insects are required for laboratory examination, the methods used for pest eradication will almost certainly be unsuitable. Traps able to catch insects alive are invaluable here. Traps can also be adapted so that they incorporate various trial insecticides and provide a means for monitoring the effectiveness of these.

Pitfall Insect Traps

These are simple but effective traps for capturing ground-moving insects such as cockroaches, crickets, grasshoppers, earwigs, beetles and certain bugs.

Empty containers such as glass jars, cans or plastic boxes can be used on their own, provided that they are deep enough to prevent insects from escaping by jumping out and have slippery sides to prevent them from climbing out; but used in this way one has to rely upon insects tumbling in by chance. The game of chance can be loaded much more heavily in the trap-owner's favour if some extra provisions are made.

Baits can be added to the jars. Many insects are attracted by baits including sugar solution, made by boiling granulated sugar in water at a rate of 4oz (114g) of sugar to $\frac{1}{4}$ pint (175ml) of water. Raw molasses can similarly be used. Insects caught in these traps would eventually drown; if they are wanted alive the bait in the bottom of the jar can be covered with wire gauze or perforated galvanized sheeting, so that the bait odour can escape but the insects stay on the platform (see Figure 41).

This idea can be carried a stage further with some insects, notably ground beetles (*Carabidae*), rove beetles (*Staphylinidae*), weevils (*Curculionidae*) and scavenger beetles (*Hydrophilidae*). A solution of formaldehyde (methanal) is used in the bottom of a jar which is sunk until its mouth is at ground level. The solution is doubly useful for not only will it attract insects of the above types, but when they have fallen into the jar it also serves as a killer and preservative. Provided that the insects are not required alive, but are needed for examination, at least by using this method they will not decompose as they would do in water or in sugar solution; in fact sugar solution can be worse than water because it will eventually ferment and produce a growth of moulds. On the other hand, 'aged' sugar solution can be useful in certain circumstances for attracting different kinds of insects from those it would attract when it is fresh.

Experiments by Cox using formaldehyde solution showed that

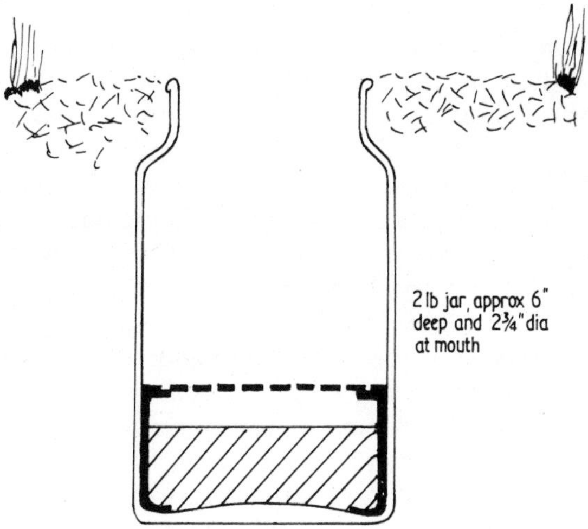

Fig 41 Pitfall trap showing gauze platform

it was effective in pitfall traps not only for insects, but also for other invertebrate animals, such as spiders, millipedes, woodlice and harvestmen.

There are other kinds of baits: for example, houseflies and many other types of flies are attracted by stale beer. This also attracts wasps, and has the advantage that it does not attract honey bees—which although they can sting are not considered as pests.

Dung beetles are so-called because they feed upon dung and this can be used as a bait to catch them in pitfall traps. Carrion beetles will be attracted to traps in which a small dead bird or mammal is decomposing.

When using pitfall traps it is important to observe a number of precautions. Greenslade, in an experiment using glass jars, showed that the best catch was in jars sunk to their rims in the ground, with the surrounding area cleared of vegetation. If vegetation was left it often fouled the mouth of the jar and reduced the catch. A jar that is not sunk into the ground might take insects crawling on the vegetation, but these are seldom as numerous as those crawling on the ground.

Care must be taken to ensure that pitfall traps cannot fill with rainwater, which might dilute or neutralize the bait. It might also fill to overflowing and float out the catch—unimportant if the trap is only intended for pests, but frustrating for an operator who is carrying out a research programme where the catch is needed for examination. The remedy is to use covers over the traps. These must be sufficiently heavy not to blow away, such as a solid block of wood, a flat stone or an old clay floor tile. The cover must be supported, to protect the mouth of the jar and yet not obstruct it in a way that prevents insects from falling in. The supports should be high enough to allow insects to crawl under but prevent insect-feeding animals such as frogs, toads or lizards from getting at the catch (see Figure 42).

If pitfall traps are being used in research, they should, as in other multiple-trap exercises, be distributed on some kind of grid pattern within the area of investigation. Bearing in mind the nature of the terrain and the likely density of the insects, one can decide on a suitable interval distance in the grid. If sampling is to be carried out on several sites, the same pattern should be used on each occasion, especially if the results from different sites are to be compared.

Traps should be examined reasonably frequently if a total catch is to be analysed, because carnivorous captives may well feed on the less aggressive forms and thereby give an inaccurate picture of the true situation.

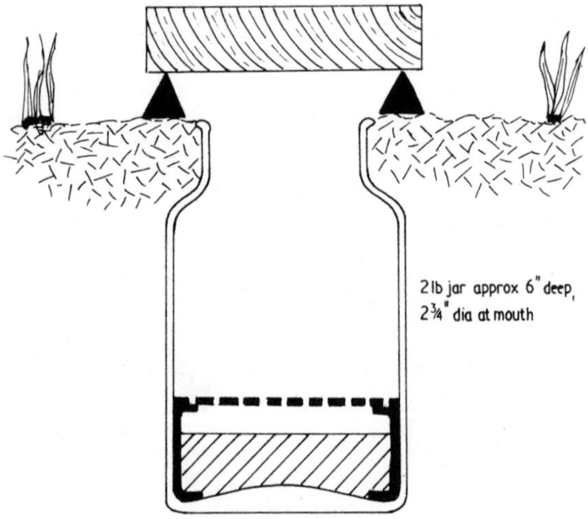

Fig 42 Protecting the mouth of a pitfall trap

Light Traps

In 1950 two brothers, H. S. and P. J. Robinson, wrote of experiments they had conducted to establish the reason for the apparent attraction of insects to a light source. Light traps had long been established, but if they were to be improved to capture insects on a selective basis, the reasons why the insects were attracted needed to be understood.

Briefly, insects are affected by the power of a source of light. As the power is increased, more insects of the same species will be attracted. An increase in surface brightness, which is the power for a given surface area, will attract a wider range of species.

It is also important to appreciate that there are two zones surrounding a source of light. Insects are sensitive to the light in the outer zone because it is picked up by their eyes; they are aware of the light, but it does not necessarily attract them and they can pass out of its influence. The inner zone, however, will usually deflect an insect from its normal flight path towards the light. There are exceptions to this: weakly flying insects, especially, may actually be repelled by the light from high-intensity sources (Verheijen, 1960).

The wavelength of light may also be significant. Various authorities have shown that some species of biting flies are caught more easily in light traps which, in addition to visible light, also emit ultraviolet light. Other species may be caught by so-called 'black lights', that is, those which emit *only* ultraviolet light. More recently it has been shown that species such as the mosquito *Aedes aegypti* L, which is not attracted by white light, can be attracted by infra-red light.

This may seem to be very academic, but when light traps are being used to sample a mosquito-ridden swamp in a tropical country, the use of different light sources to establish which species are present can be of tremendous importance medically, because of the part played by mosquitoes in transmitting disease-causing organisms.

Sheeting

This is the simplest form of light trap, still handy when other kinds of traps are not available. All that is required is a white sheet either placed flat on the ground or suspended vertically—it must hang with a fold on the ground surface so that falling insects are easily seen. Any portable light source can be used in conjunction with the sheet, such as a battery-operated electric lamp, a bottled-gas lamp or a kerosene lamp.

The disadvantage of using sheeting is that the operator must stand by throughout, in order to capture insects as they land on the sheet, otherwise they will crawl away into shadows and obscurity.

Other early forms of light traps suffered the same problem of having shadow cones into which insects could move to escape the influence of the light.

Mercury Vapour Light Traps

The Robinson brothers devised a trap to overcome the problem of shade cones, by using a mercury vapour lamp, which also gives an extremely intense light. These traps have been used extensively for taking night-flying moths.

The Robinson trap is seen in Figure 43. The base is a shallow metal drum. Above it is fixed an inverted cone of transparent plastic, open at the top to take a metal funnel which has vertical metal vanes. The MV lamp is placed between the vanes. It has three pins, so requires an appropriate lampholder, which overcomes the possibility of putting the lamp into a normal socket. The MV lamp has a choke which regulates the brightness level,

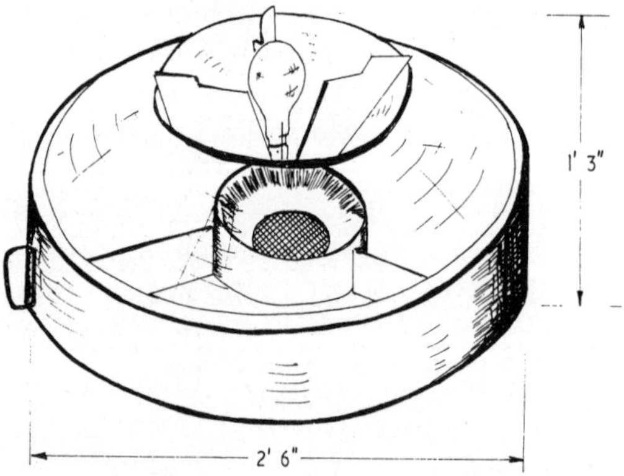

Fig 43 The Robinson light trap

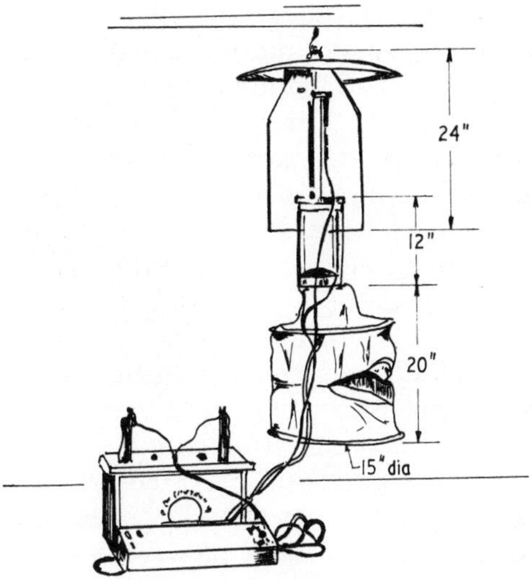

Fig 44 The Monks Wood trap

otherwise it would burn out, as the self-generating mercury ions, if unchecked, would produce an ever-increasing current. In practice the source of power is usually a portable electrical generator, which should have an on–off timeswitch.

The moths are attracted by the lamp and spiral down towards it, eventually flying around it. The shade cones within the vanes of the funnel provide baffles against which the moths collide, and then they drop into the trap below. The drum base usually contains broken pieces of fibre board, of the kind used by egg distributors as egg trays, and these encourage the moths to settle.

Refinements in Light Traps

Since the Robinsons designed their trap, numerous variations have appeared. One of these is known as a Monks Wood Light trap and is based upon an earlier version called the Pennsylvania trap, except that like yet another, the CDC Trap, it incorporates a small electric fan which draws the catch into a collecting bag. The Monks Wood trap, seen in Figure 44, was devised at the Monks Wood Experimental Station, part of what is now the Institute of Terrestrial Ecology at Abbots Ripton in Cambridgeshire, England. It was intended especially for sampling populations of mosquitoes. Apart from the fan, which is particularly useful when trapping small flies, this trap has the further advantage of lamp interchangeability, allowing for light of different wavelengths and therefore different species selection.

The trap consists of three main sections. The upper section houses the lamp, which is a 9in (230mm) 6-watt actinic fluorescent tube vertically mounted between three white plastic vanes. The tubes can emit black light, ultraviolet light or white light of varying spectral power distribution, according to type. The source of power is usually a 12-volt d.c. car battery which operates through a transistor ballast box. The box incorporates a transistorized photosensitive cell which will switch on the light automatically at sunset and off at sunrise, although there is a bypass switch which will allow the trap to be operated at other times if desired.

The light section vanes slot into the middle section, which is a tube of clear acrylic plastic 7½in (190mm) high and 4in (100mm)

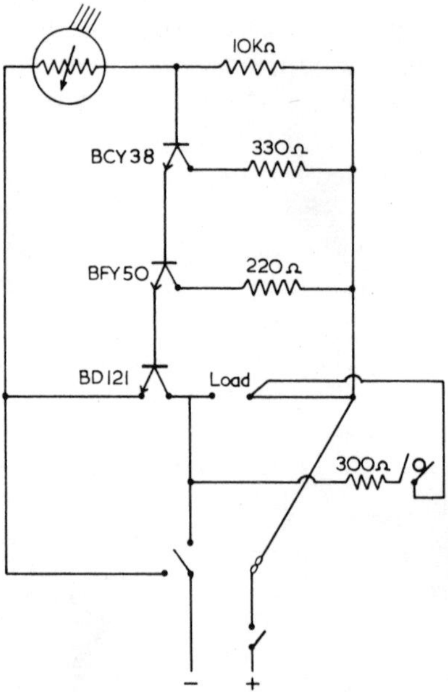

Fig 45 Circuit diagram for Monks Wood trap

in diameter with walls ¼in (6mm) thick. A metal ring secured by clips screwed to the tube walls at the mouth end can hold a removable wire-mesh screen, whereas at the base of the tube is screwed a motor on which is mounted a 3in (75mm) aluminium fan. Under the motor is a 3 to 4½-volt d.c. unit with an in-series resistor of 3,000 ohm, 0.5 watt connected to the 12-volt battery (see circuit diagram in Figure 45).

The third part of the trap is the collecting bag, the neck of which contains an elastic tape to grip around a groove cut into the base of the acrylic tube. The bag has its top and upper walls of cloth and the lower walls and base of mosquito-proof netting. There is a slit around a third of the middle section of the bag wall and this has a Velcro-type fastening. Damp plastic sponge can be put through this and placed in the bottom of the bag, to keep the trapped insects alive while the trap is left unattended. An inverted plastic funnel in the base of the bag prevents captured insects from escaping.

In wet weather the trap can be protected by a metal shield placed over the top of the plastic vanes, while the ballast box and battery can be covered with polythene bags. A fully charged battery will keep the trap running for about thirty-six hours, giving four average nights' usage.

When used by Service for sampling African populations of mosquitoes, Monks Wood traps were placed either in village huts or in the flight paths of mosquitoes between their breeding places and the villages.

The incorporation of the fan ensures that species repelled by bright light when in its immediate vicinity will, none the less, be sucked in since they are also usually weak fliers.

These traps, while eminently suitable for catching mosquitoes, especially attracting inflying ones within huts before they can feed on the sleeping occupants, will also catch other flies such as *Simulium* or Tipulids (craneflies). When tested in England, a trap captured moths, beetles and bugs, so it obviously has a versatility beyond the purpose for which it was designed.

These traps can be suspended from trees or from a stretched line at varying heights, which gives them a greater opportunity for sampling different insect-occupying niches than would be possible with a ground-resting trap of the Robinson type.

Fan Traps

Insects can also be caught in fan traps without the use of light, but incorporating other attracting materials. This was found possible in the case of blood-sucking flies of the species *Simulium*. Since these flies suck the blood of birds and mammals it seemed likely that some particular feature of the body of the host was the attractant. Four Canadian scientists (Fallis, Bennett, Griggs and Allen) used fan traps beside which carbon dioxide gas was released. This followed observations that large numbers of these black flies were caught at the end of hoses down which a man exhaled his breath.

The fan traps were cylinders 5in (127mm) long and 4in (101mm) diameter and had four 3in (76mm) blades rotated by a 6 volt motor. Gauze collecting bags were tied to the bases of the traps. The traps were suspended from the ends of 12ft (3.6m) arms extended from a turntable which was rotated through 90 degrees every two minutes. Varying amounts of carbon dioxide gas were released near to some traps, but there were experimental controls with no gas release. Similarly the air near to some traps was heated to simulate the effect of body heat released into the air. The results of this work showed that significantly more black flies were caught by traps associated with released carbon dioxide and heat. Heat on its own had relatively little effect, but traps with carbon dioxide alone were more effective than traps without carbon dioxide. It might be argued that heat and carbon dioxide are not factors responsible for attracting insects, but for activating them, thus bringing them more readily under the influence of the suction force of the fans. Whatever the explanation the effectiveness is not in dispute, although it must be stressed that different species of flies will react in different ways.

The purpose of these accounts is to illustrate the necessity, when using insect traps for scientific experiments, of considering the use of attracting substances that demonstrate properties significant in the lives of the insects being trapped. During the hours of darkness light is obviously important, but during the daytime chemical substances may be more effective.

Adhesive Traps

The small size and light weight of most insects renders them vulnerable to capture on sticky surfaces, but if these also have in-built attractiveness then the combination produces the ideal trap.

Many readers will have had the experience of going to an unsealed can of molasses or a jar of fruit preserve, or even an opened can of condensed milk, only to find a seething mass of black sugar ants stuck on the surface. No doubt if you have an ant problem and are prepared to sacrifice a jar or two of these delicacies, they will perform as ready-made and perfectly adequate traps.

'Sugaring' is an insect-trapping method which has been employed for a very long time. Moth collectors have found it a very useful way of capturing the night-flying types, but this by no means excludes the use of sugaring during the daytime. The basic requirements for sugaring are a solution of fermented sugar and a suitable surface on which to paint it. Artificial surfaces can be made from pieces of board, tin, plastic or glass, but there is no reason at all why the bait should not be put on tree trunks, fencing posts or the wooden sides of buildings; in fact the natural surface may already be used by resting insects.

Most collectors have their own recipes for the sugar bait, often the result of experimenting with various formulas until they find one that is successful for them and for the species they are after. In this respect collectors are often like cooks: the recipe that works for one may be completely useless for another, even in the same situation. There is no scientific explanation for this, but it is a fact of life.

A suitable mixture with which to start is obtained by boiling together 2 lb (1 kg) of granulated sugar, 1 lb (500 g) of treacle (molasses), half a pint of beer and a few drops of rum. When the mixture has reached a sticky consistency or has acquired a flavour judged to be suitable (tasting should stop at some point before collapsing on the floor), the product can be cooled and then painted on the surfaces to be used as traps.

The method of choosing suitable sites will depend upon the collector having some knowledge of the habits of the insects he is collecting. Generally it is wise to remember that traps must be visited regularly and therefore a circular route will be the least time consuming. If there are no natural surfaces available, as might happen in an open grassland area or around an open stretch of water, the bait would have to be painted on artificial surfaces which would then be stuck into the ground so that the odours of fermentation are carried downwind.

When insects must not be damaged because they are being taken in order to build up a scientific collection, they should be detached by means of an aspirator from the trap surface. A suitable apparatus is shown in Figure 46 and can be operated either by sucking with the mouth or by using a rubber suction bulb. The collected insects should not be killed immediately but left for a day or two in order that ingested sugar can be digested and the waste products expelled. Failure to allow this would result in poorly preserved specimens.

When experimenting with fan traps Fallis, and others already referred to, discovered that black flies were attracted in large numbers to sticky human manikins. In this instance the sticky substance had no inherent attractive features for the flies; they were responding to the visual forms of the human body which, had they been real, would have been a source of blood for them to suck. As with the fan trap experiments, the attraction increased when carbon dioxide gas was released at the side of the manikins, because this gave a simulation of exhaled human breath.

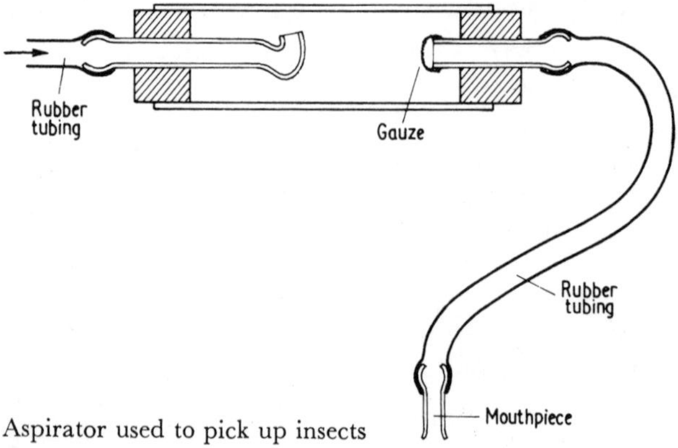

Fig 46 Aspirator used to pick up insects

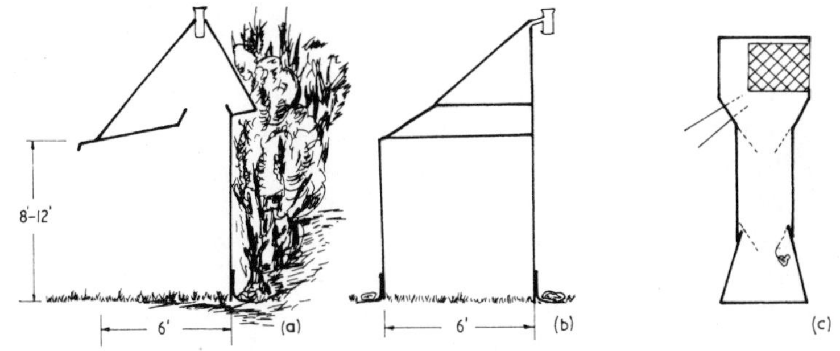

Fig 47 A Malaise trap

At one time the only way of combating the summer seasonal plague of houseflies was to use sticky flypapers. These are still available, usually in country areas, and they are very effective, if you have no objection to a piece of gummy paper hanging from a ceiling and gradually blackening with accumulating flies. In fact although they may be unpleasant visually, they may be a lot safer than some of the aerosol insecticides with which we are in danger of polluting our atmosphere to health-hazard proportions. Home-made flypapers can be produced by painting paper strips with a heated mixture of spruce gum and linseed oil.

Before concluding this section, attention should be given to the naturally occurring adhesive substances that can serve as natural traps. These include the resinous exudates from trees, especially those of the conifer type, and the sugary products which ooze out of ripening fruits. Insect collectors should be aware of these likely places in which to find specimens and keep an eye open for them.

Miscellaneous Insect Traps

The first trap to be included here is the Malaise trap. It was designed by Dr Rene Malaise, a Swede, and still proves useful, despite being non-selective, for capturing flying and crawling insects. The principle upon which it works is related to the instinctive reaction of insects to fly or move upwards after they have fed.

The trap also depends upon the natural tendency for insects to move into shade which in this case is provided by a tent. The base of the trap is formed from mosquito netting on three sides of a square, leaving the fourth side open to a height of 12ft (3.6m). The sides of the base are 6ft (1.8m) across and above it (see Figure 47) is a pyramid-shaped roof into which insects can enter through a baffle funnel. There is a killing bottle at the apex of the pyramid which is usually made from brass and is in three sections. The bottle screws on to a threaded socket at the top of the pyramid and its three sections are separated from each other by downward-projecting funnels. The top section has a wire-mesh grill for admitting daylight while the bottom one contains an anaesthetic such as ethyl acetate or a killing fluid such as alcohol.

The insects are attracted by the shade in the tent and move inside to crawl up the walls. Eventually they enter the killing bottle where, in the middle section, they come under the influence of the anaesthetic. This works slowly as they are moving towards the grill, but eventually they are overcome and drop back to undergo complete anaesthetization. They drop into the bottom compartment and if this contains ethyl acetate they can remain in this for several days relaxed ready for setting. If there is alcohol in the bottom it will kill them and also preserve them indefinitely until the bottle is emptied.

The best situation for this trap is one where it can capture insects flying up-wind, by having the open side facing down-wind. To guard against the possibility of a change in the wind direction it is advisable to use a double trap. This has a double base section with openings facing in opposite directions, but these are linked to a common roof and a single killing bottle.

Apart from accounting for the wind direction the traps should be positioned close to a likely source of insects, such as against a hedgerow or shrubbery, within a highly scented flower border or on the edge of a pond or lake.

In the author's previous book on animal traps mention was made of a formalin trap designed by the British Museum (Natural History) for catching flies. While effective, more recent knowledge of the danger to human health of even quite small concentrations of formaldehyde (as little as two parts per million in the atmosphere) suggests that it should no longer be recommended.

For catching aerial insects, including all kinds of flies, the battery-operated radiant-energy traps are very efficient. Black

techniques involved that they could refine the process to one of almost certainty in getting catches.

Trapping under these conditions can be greatly improved by having a good background knowledge of animal behaviour. This is further developed by having some idea of the types of animals likely to be found in different areas throughout the world. An appreciation of the kinds of animals likely to be active at night, either foraging for vegetation or hunting for prey, would be very useful as this is also a time when a unit may conceal itself for a rest period and have at least a short time in which to wait near to traps.

Those animals which are active during the day frequently visit waterholes at daybreak or at sunset and traps set either on the trails leading to the water or in the shallow waters of the edge may be particularly effective. Included among the animals considered here are antelopes, deer, members of the pig family and wild cattle. It should also be remembered that animal predators are as much aware of these habits of their prey as we are. In the event that trapping is going on in an area where one might expect to find large carnivores, particularly members of the cat family, it is as well to be ready to find the trapped prey already taken by their natural enemies. Alternatively, when a trapper is visiting traps to recover the catch some caution is necessary to make sure that he is not overtaken by events and is himself trapped when a carnivore comes along on the same errand.

Trapping for survival has another aspect of importance, namely the size of the animals being trapped. While a large animal may feed a lot of people, it would have to be skinned and jointed if a unit were on the move in order to break it down into portable portions. By and large, the bigger animals have relatively less flesh compared with the amount of bone which would be an additional weight to carry with only limited resource value. Smaller animals may be carried away in pockets and packs immediately and dealt with later, leaving no evidence of a bivouac. However, it is always worth while paunching animals to increase the keeping quality, and the entrails can either be buried or kept for baiting other traps.

The subject of baiting is an important one, because it is unlikely that some of the favourite concoctions used by professional trappers would be on hand. Of necessity there would have to be recourse to naturally available materials. Apart from the entrails and offal from dead animals to attract carnivores, a knowledge of local vegetation and the use of fruits would be significant in capturing vegetable- and fruit-eating animals such as hares, rabbits, monkeys, opossums, squirrels and many birds. The animals which are attracted by the products of their own scent glands, musks, urine and faeces are not usually first choices as food, so that trapping foxes, badgers, skunks, jackals, wild dogs and hunting dogs will not receive priority treatment and the skill required for extracting natural scent baits from dead animals would not be important. None the less, if there was little else that could easily be trapped a bunch of hungry men would be unlikely to turn squeamish when faced with no better alternative.

In the context of war the problems of concealment, keeping on the move and covering up traces of camps are all essential and add to the difficulties in trapping, but there might well be a place for trapping in other kinds of emergencies. Many places are still very remote and a surprisingly large number of survivors from aircraft wrecks and forced landings have been marooned in difficult country, short of provisions and with no means of contacting the outside world. If rescue is a long time arriving, the ability to trap animals for food could be a life-saving resource. It is true that people have survived on seeds and fruit, but such a diet often causes unfortunate reactions from the digestive system.

Similarly, expeditions to uninhabited and remote parts of the world often meet problems. They may have organized their provisions carefully, but disaster often strikes when least expected and a sudden tropical rainstorm followed by flooding could easily carry away all the supplies. Animals have sometimes entered a temporarily deserted base camp and made free with the food.

There are probably many more situations like these, where survival may be assisted by an elementary knowledge of the principles of trapping. Meanwhile, ostrich like, we shun the possibility of a future war on a worldwide scale, but such a catastrophe could terminate in situations of the kind portrayed on television series when remnants of civilizations struggle for survival.

Constructing Simple Traps

The raw materials required for building traps under survival conditions must possess some simple but essential properties. Weights are required for the construction of deadfall traps and they must be heavy enough to kill an animal on which they fall. The weight must relate to the animal to be trapped and generally speaking the larger the animal, the heavier the weight will need to be. To kill, a weight must crush a skull, break a back or crush a chest. The action and effect can be amplified by increasing the height from which the weight is to fall, as it is not the weight alone which kills but the force with which it strikes its victim. Force is the combination of weight and the acceleration with which it moves when falling, so it stands to reason that the greater the distance through which the weight moves the more it will accelerate. This must be remembered when it is necessary to kill a large animal using a deadfall trap and the only available weight appears to be too small.

The obvious materials for use as deadfall weights are rocks and baulks of timber, but there may be other items available if an army unit is covering ground left by a retreating enemy.

Some form of noose is frequently used as part of a trap system and the simplest example is of a plain noose or snare. Of all the traps that have been used, except perhaps the pitfall, the snare is likely to be the oldest. Snares have been made from all manner of materials and in the hands of skilled trappers they can be both effective and humane. In the hands of the inexperienced they can be vicious and unsuccessful.

To be effective as a snare the noose must have an easy-running slip-knot and this will be aided by using a material which is uniformly smooth over the full length of its run. When cord or wire is not available, natural plant fibres or the sinews of animals can work very well—after all these were the materials from which the first snares were made. However, except for large animals, particularly those with long legs, animal sinews will be short; they are also elastic and can be stretched, but this must be done carefully or else they will snap. When they have been stretched they must be dried, but they should not be allowed to get too brittle and should be rubbed with animal fat or plant oil.

A good snare should have a stop if an animal is not to be caught in a manner that will kill it outright. Using a stop means that there is a limited extent for the slip-knot to travel, enough to hold the animal but not so tightly as to chafe its skin. Similarly, some kind of pulley or swivel device at the point where the snare is to be anchored to the ground by a peg will prevent chafing, regardless of the direction in which an animal struggles to free itself. It is not too much to ask that human survival should not be at the expense of animal suffering. Pulleys can be made from the ends of the limb bones of deer, antelope, goats or sheep.

The advantage of the snare is its portability, unlike most other traps. Snares can be thrust into the pocket so that they are always with you, taking up little space and always ready for action.

Plant fibres can be produced from green springy saplings. The bark is peeled and immediately underneath this there are usually soft white woody fibres. These can be peeled off too and cut into narrow strips, which, if carefully rubbed between the palms of the hands, will become soft and pliable, yet quite strong. When they are dry they can be oiled or greased to make a slip-knot run easily. Animals of the horse family with long-haired tails will produce ideal snare material. A long tail hair can be bent double and then twisted, leaving the first ½in (13mm) to form a loop. The loose ends are threaded together through the loop and fastened to an anchor peg, so forming a very strong and extremely efficient snare.

When sinews and plant fibres are being used, there may be difficulty in getting even thicknesses over long lengths to provide for easy-running knots, especially if time to prepare the materials is short. In this situation a substitute must be found for a slip-knot and an old Eskimo device can be copied; this used the shaft of a small long bone—the hollow leg bone from a bird would do—and one end of the snare is fastened through a hole made in the end of the bone. The snare cord is then drawn through the hollow bone and fastened to an anchor stake. Exactly the same effect can be achieved by using a brass or plastic eyelet hole from a boot, except that the end of the snare cord is tied around the pulley rim of the eyelet.

Traditionally, certainly in Britain, snares have been called 'wires', especially among the poaching fraternity. Wire is an ideal material, preferably of twisted brass, and among the items that a survival unit might possess, this is one that would certainly serve a useful purpose for trapping. If stranded wire is to be used it is an advantage to be able to splice the ends to form a loop.

In conjunction with snares it is sometimes beneficial to use a spring; in fact there is a category of traps called spring snares. The spring usually takes the form of a springy piece of wood which can be produced from young trees at the sapling stage. The whole sapling can be bent over to produce a reasonably well-anchored spring, but short lengths can be employed as part of a trap made from pieces of wood put together in the form of a box. Snares inside the box are released when a trigger is activated by an animal entering the box and the springy wood supplies the tension.

For many of these traps various forms of triggers and release catches are necessary, but normally they can be fashioned from short lengths of not too stout tree branch. They are suitably notched by a whittling knife, or left with a shortened projecting side-branch to catch against a notch elsewhere. In the event of there being short lengths of iron or steel rod available, the ends can be sharpened on a rock and then used as nails driven into a tree trunk as part of a trigger release system. The necessity for baits has been mentioned and often these are stuck on to bait sticks, which are used, often as part of the triggering system, in the kinds of traps included in this section.

The ways in which all the materials and devices mentioned here are used will become apparent when the trapping systems are described and the illustrations examined.

Survival Trapping in the Field

By adopting a logical order which in some ways recapitulates the early history of trap development, the first trap that can be used for survival situations is the pitfall trap. In its simplest form it is a hole in the ground, with an area sufficiently large to take the size of animal that a trail and the examination of its tracks would suggest, and with a depth great enough to prevent its escape after it has tumbled in.

Animal trails must be recognizable and the signs left on the trail interpreted. A worn pathway might be from the movement of local people in a populated area, but whether in mud, dust or sand it should not be too difficult to identify human footprints as distinct from those of wild animals. A knowledge of the kinds of prints left by hoofed animals, cloven-hoofed animals and pad-footed animals is essential, while the distance apart of these related to their size on a track will tell if an animal has been running or moving slowly. Although most animals can usually thread their way quite silently through thick undergrowth in forests, an animal in flight may crash through leaving a trail of broken twigs and fallen leaves. Signs of cropped grass indicate grazing animals and chewed leaves indicate the browsers. This kind of information is of extreme value when siting traps and estimating the size that is required. Animals' droppings can also provide proof of the kind and size of creatures in an area and the freshness will show how recently they were there. The remains of animal carcases will indicate the presence of predators or scavengers, and the way that the carcase has been eaten may suggest a particular kind of animal.

When siting a pitfall trap, or indeed any other kind of trap, careful interpretation of the field evidence on animal trails will make the task easier.

Pitfall traps should be camouflaged, as far as is possible, to eradicate any signs of interference with the trail. To do the job properly requires care and one of the scarcest commodities in a survival situation, time. In this situation the best that time allows should be the target. When a pit has been dug, it should be covered with enmeshed sticks, strong enough to support some form of covering material, but not so strong that they prevent an animal from falling into the pit. If time allows and the trail is grassy, the covering could be of thin turf. If the trail is of loose ground, a preliminary cover of grass or broad leaves would then allow for soil or sand to be poured over. Sticks or branches from trees can be used either side of the pit to serve as a lead-in and to restrict animal movement to a direction over the pit. The primitive practice of putting sharpened staves in the ground at the bottom of the pit could be used in an attempt to kill an animal, but this is a somewhat barbaric method and one more likely to injure an animal than to kill it. If firearms and ammunition are available much the more efficient way is to shoot a captive; if silencer-fitted weapons are available there would be no disturbance to other forms of wildlife and no exposure of a unit's position. Of course with this kind of equipment it might be considered prudent to lie in wait and shoot the animal without worrying about a trap, but this does require vigilance whereas the pit will work without surveillance.

Pitfall traps can also be constructed in ice-covered water as well as solid ground, if there is a sufficient depth of ice to provide a solid bottom—otherwise the captured animals would simply float away under the ice. Such pits could be used for arctic foxes and, if big enough, for reindeer and bears.

Lieutenant-Colonel Bruce Donald has drawn attention to a pitfall trap which uses pivoted boards over the top. Set on a trail and lightly covered with soil it could be most effective, although it was designed to fit under a gap in a dry stone wall (see Fig 48).

Deadfall Traps

These can be used for animals of all sizes and the weight can be of wood or rock.

One of the oldest and still one of the most effective is the Figure 4 trap. It is useful for small animals of all kinds, both birds and

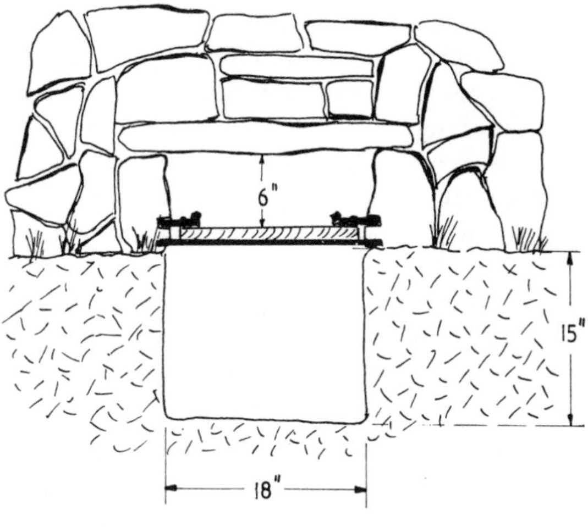

Fig 48 Pivot-board pitfall trap

Fig 49 Figure 4 trap

mammals, and, like the snare, has the possibility of being carried around in a pocket, so that at a trapping site it is only necessary to find a suitable weight. As seen in Figure 49, the basic elements of the trap are three pieces of wood. They can be made from old packing-case material or straight pieces of tree branch. The central horizontal unit is the bait bar which has the appropriate bait fastened or hung at one end. A notch is cut in the side at the centre point and at two-thirds of the distance to the other end a further notch is cut into the top. There is a vertical stick which has a notch at its centre, such that this and the notch on the bait bar lock together. Thus the lower edge of the notch in the upright must be at 90 degrees to the surface. To hold these two bars in equilibrium the third stick has one end pointed by cutting it off at an angle and this fits in the notch towards the end of the bait bar. The end of the upright is similarly sharpened to fit into a notch made a short distance from the end of the third stick. When carefully and delicately set up, with a flat stone or a log with a flattened edge resting on the top of the third stick, the whole should remain in position without collapsing until an animal pulls at the bait. It follows that the bait end of the horizontal bar must be well under the weight, otherwise the natural recoil of an animal as the trap collapses would take it out of harm's way. This kind of trap is set on a trail or anywhere that animals congregate

—near to water, for example, or, in the case of birds, where seeds are scattered on the ground. Camouflage is not necessary as the bait should provide an attraction sufficient enough to overcome an animal's fear of strange objects.

Deadfalls can be set to catch animals on trails, the so-called trail-set deadfall. Some kind of cord is essential to hold a weight suspended from a tree branch overhanging a trail and this could be produced from sinews or plant fibres as already described, if string or wire is not available.

It is important to use a trigger which allows the weight to drop when it is moved by an animal. The trigger can be baited (see Figure 50a) or it can be part of a trip system as seen in Figure 50b. The stone is tied to one end of a cord and the other end is thrown over a suitable tree branch. The weight is hauled up to a convenient height and then the free end of the cord is attached to the trigger. With a baited trigger the pull on this releases the weight, but with the trip mechanism, the free end of the cord is carried over the bar held between two guides driven into the base of the tree trunk, carried across the trail at a convenient height and fastened to an anchoring post on the other side.

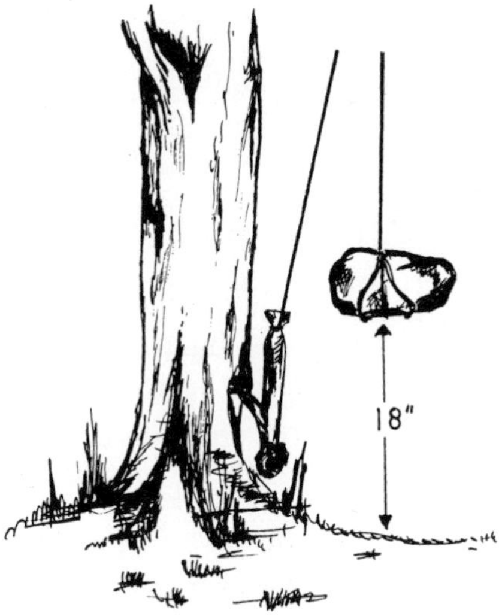

Fig 50a Baited trigger deadfall trap

Fig 50b Trip-cord deadfall trap

Knowing the size of an animal to be trapped is most important, firstly to judge the height at which the weight must be suspended and secondly to estimate the position of the neck or middle-back regions on which the weight should fall. If the weight falls on the rump end, the heavy bone structure and muscular padding will dissipate the killing effect of the weight.

Trappers should appreciate that an animal that they injure, apart from any suffering it may experience, can often be dangerous to a greater degree than is normal as a result of pain. If a piece of sharpened metal can be found and is knocked into a heavy log, the exposed end can also be sharpened and the whole structure used as a harpoon deadfall, combining weight with a spearing action. These trail-set deadfall traps can be camouflaged to some extent, particularly where there is a trip-cord, by masking the cord and anchor stake with vegetation. The bait stick of the other version really needs no disguise, although a lead-in to it on a wide trail could be beneficial.

Using a log, the size of which can be adjusted to the size of the animal to be caught, a pole deadfall trap can be set up. As seen in Figure 51, it consists of two parts, the deadfall section and the cage with the bait. The trap is best set up close to an animal track, but preferably up against the base of a large tree or against the face of a wall or cliff. The cage is built from sticks and rocks, with loose vegetation to provide cover. The sides consist of sticks about 30in (760mm) long and these are pushed 14in (355mm) into the ground with the spaces in between filled with flat rocks. Other sticks form beams across the top and the whole is roofed in with leafy branches and long grass. The cage should be about 1ft (300mm) square for animals the size of stoats and mongoose and appropriately larger for foxes, badgers or similarly sized creatures.

The deadfall is made from a heavy log which is notched at one end to fit against an anchor stick and so prevented from slipping backwards. It is tilted upwards across the mouth of the cage and has four guide sticks, two either side, to direct its fall. If the ground underneath is soft, a flat rock or a flat piece of wood should be buried level with the ground surface, providing a more efficient killing platform than would be the case if the log fell on to soft ground.

The log is held up by a prop stick, but a bait stick, which points backwards into the cage, comes between the prop and the log. A suitable bait is hung inside the cage from the bait stick. When an animal is attracted by the bait it is unable to reach it from the side because of the cage, so it has to reach in under the log. It may move the prop, in which case it will release the log and this will

Fig 51 Pole deadfall trap

fall and strike its head; otherwise, if it negotiates the prop, when it pulls on the bait the bait stick releases the prop and the log will strike its back.

Before leaving the deadfall traps, the so-called English brick deadfall is another example to consider. As seen in Figure 52, it is made from four bricks, but careful adaptation of the principle is perfectly possible using logs instead. Three bricks or logs form three sides of a cage and the fourth is propped up between the two parallel sides. Bait is sprinkled inside the cage, mainly to catch birds; when the bait is being taken it only requires a slight movement against the prop to bring the central brick down. If the edge of the brick catches the top of the cross-brick the animal will be trapped alive, but if the edge clears the cross-brick there will be an authentic deadfall action.

Snares

The simple snare can be used by itself across a trail, in a gap in the vegetation through which animals pass, at the mouth of a burrow from which animals will emerge or at the mouth of a tree-hollow which may be used as a shelter. They can also be used in land drains, where these exist, to catch small burrowing animals which use drainage systems as tunnels.

The advantages of snares in survival trapping, especially in an area which might contain belligerent forces, are silence in action, speed when they are skilfully set and an absence of blood to provide tell-tale evidence.

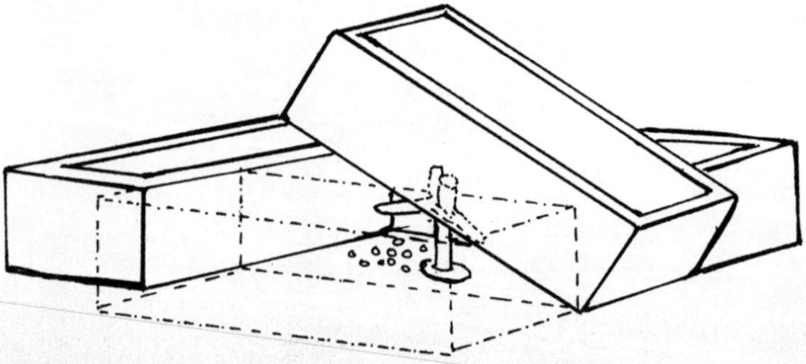

Fig 52 English brick deadfall trap

Fig 53 Carolina hanging snare

They are of most use in trapping animals with long necks because the tightening noose cannot be jerked free, also the chance of killing such animals humanely is likely because the neck can more easily be broken by the combined forces of a bolting animal and a tightening snare.

Animals without long necks are more likely to be caught in a snare set to trap the feet, but this is often inhumane unless the trapper is on hand to kill the catch quickly.

The use of stops and swivels has already been mentioned and they are refinements which reduce animal suffering.

Spring Snares

Snares in combination with a spring device can provide a more effective trap and have additional advantages.

A good example which has been used in survival training for the US Forces is the Carolina Hanging Snare. As seen in Figure 53, this combines the use of a snare to catch animals such as deer and antelopes with a spring action which jerks them up into the air out of the way of ground prowling predators, which might reach the trap before the trapper does. The spring is an elastic branch or sapling which is bent over and tied to a triggering set-up, and this, in turn, is attached to the free end of the noose cord. Such a trap is normally set on a trail, but sometimes it is used with a drive on a herd, which is moved in its direction. When this happens, any lead-in construction, such as rows of stakes to narrow the path taken by a moving herd, will increase the effectiveness of the drive.

Fig 54 Pole snare

If there is no spring sapling available, but there are some rigid sticks, the Carolina snare can be replaced by a pole snare. This is mainly used for small animals about the size of a hare and consists of a tripod of stakes, securely tied at the top, across which is suspended a long pole. This takes the place of the sapling by having two-thirds of its length at the heavier end behind the tripod. In front of the tripod the end of the pole has the free end of the snare attached to it. The snare cord is looped along a groove in the middle of a piece of wood which is rounded at one end and wedge-shaped at the other. Over this wooden trigger is looped another cord which is attached to an anchor peg underneath. The snare can be set up on a trail (see Figure 54) being supported by vegetation alongside. When an animal rushes into the snare, the loop over the trigger is detached and the tension on the end of the pole is released, so it jerks the noose and the captive animal up aloft.

For animals which do not follow set runs or trails, other forms of attraction have to be used and this means baiting. The trap used is a bait-set snare and to assist with its construction a broad based tree with strong surface roots fanning out is required. In the V-shape formed from two tree roots, a small cage is built out of sticks driven into the ground. Above this a small bait board with a nail or wooden peg driven through its centre is placed so that the peg rests under two guides driven into the tree trunk (see Figure 55). The snare noose is set up in front of the cage and its free end is first tied around the bait-board peg and then goes on to be tied to the end of a bent-over springy piece of wood pushed into the ground beside the tree. The bait is attached to the bait-board and when an animal pushes its head through the noose to get the bait the board is dislodged and the tension is taken out of the spring. As the spring straightens it jerks the noose upwards and simultaneously this tightens around the animal's neck.

The portable snare (Figure 56) works on an almost identical principle, but as the name suggests it is a device which can be

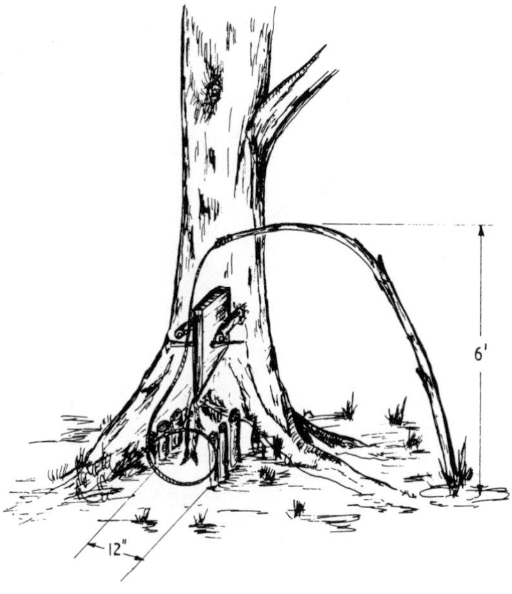

Fig 55 Bait-set snare

carried around; even quite a few would not take up much room, nor impose any great burden. Three pieces of wood are used, shaped in the manner shown in the illustration. The bait lever is fitted inside a mortice hole and hinged with a piece of wire pushed through the sides, so in fact it becomes a lever. The only requirement in addition to the pieces of wood and a snare, is a branch or sapling to form a spring. The upright of the trap is secured by string or wire to the sapling. If notches are cut into the corners of the upright where the cord is attached, there is less chance of it slipping. If cord is being used it should be wetted first and then as it dries it will grip very tightly indeed.

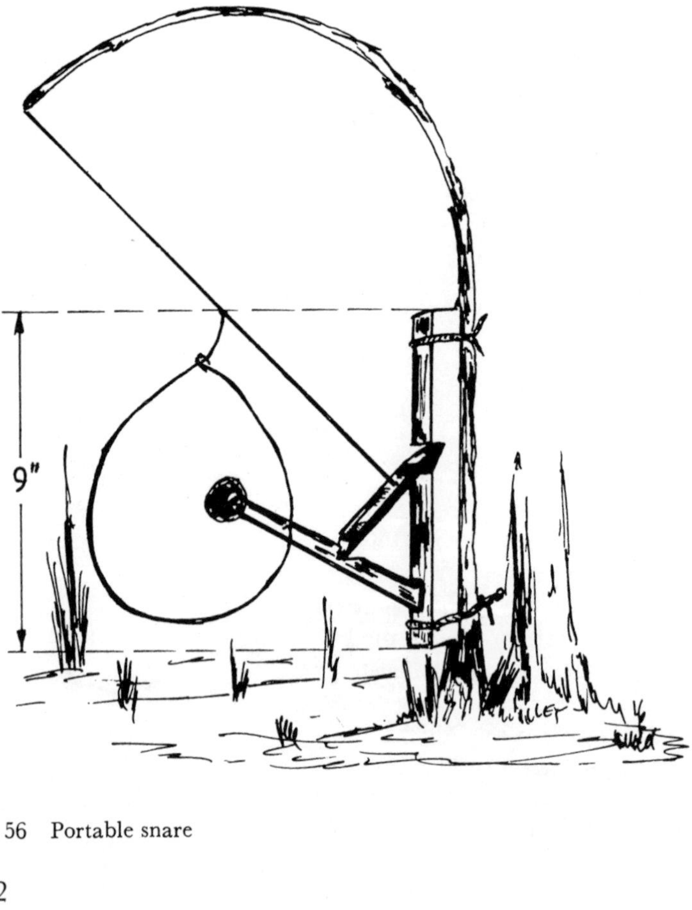

Fig 56 Portable snare

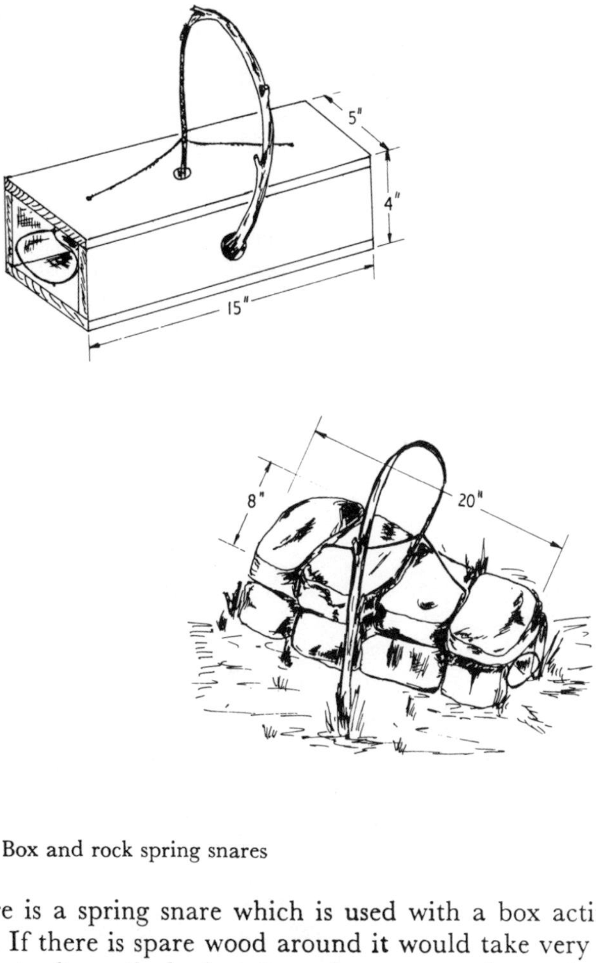

Fig 57 Box and rock spring snares

There is a spring snare which is used with a box acting as a tunnel. If there is spare wood around it would take very little to construct; alternatively, by adaptation, a natural tunnel could be made from flat rocks. The two alternatives are seen in Figure 57. The box has a springy stick pushed through a hole drilled obliquely in one side. A cord is attached to this stick and at its end is tied another cord which has two snares, one attached to each of its ends. The snares are inside the box and their drawcords pass through holes in its top. Also inside the box, at its centre, there is a trigger which may serve as a bait stick. Above it is a hole drilled through the box and it provides a means for the knotted end of the cord connecting the snares to be wedged by the trigger.

If rocks are being used the spring is forced into the ground behind the tunnel, or the tunnel could be built in front of a rooted sapling. The drawcords from the snares pass through gaps left between the rocks and the trigger and knot can be wedged between rocky slabs in the same way.

In either construction, when an animal rushes into the tunnel and dislodges the trigger it releases the knot and the spring straightens. As it does so, the nooses are jerked and tightened around the animal. With two nooses there is a double chance of holding the animal securely in the tunnel. The tunnel can be appropriately camouflaged, but care must be taken not to impede any of the cords linked with the spring stick. Such a trap can be set on a trail and will attract small inquisitive animals. It can be adapted to take animals in underground burrows where these run close to the surface. The burrow would be opened and a piece of rock or wood laid across the top to form the roof, with the rest of the trap set up as before.

The wooden box, or even a length of metal or plastic pipe, suitably drilled, could be used in water as a fish trap. It would have to be weighted to carry it downwards and keep it on the bottom, but in such a position it could catch fish such as trout, bream, tench and carp when suitable baits like freshwater mussels are used. In deep waters and where there is a current flowing, this kind of box trap could have a weight suspended from its bottom by a length of cord or wire to act as an anchor and it could be suspended in a mid-depth position by using an old oil drum as a buoy attached by another cord from the top of the box. Fish will often swim into narrow channels and movement through a tunnel of this kind would not be unduly strange for them.

Foot-trap Snare

Whereas most of the snares described so far are intended to take an animal about its head or body, preferably in a manner that will result in almost instant death by strangulation or a broken back, there is one kind of snare designed to take an animal by its foot. This, of course, produces many of the unpleasant consequences associated with the leg-hold traps. The animal is not killed immediately and unless the trapper comes quickly much

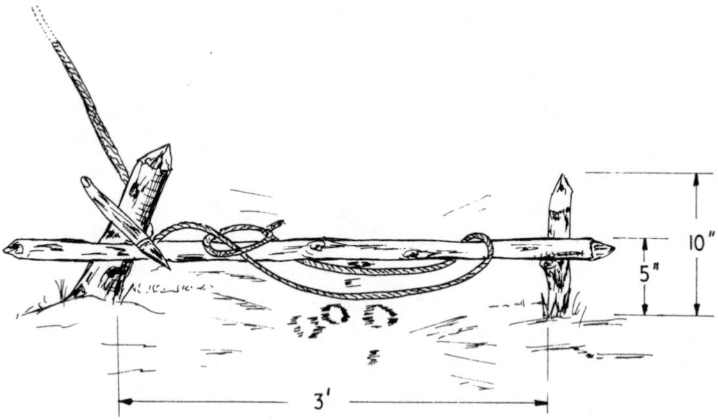

Fig 58 Foot-trap snare

suffering would occur as it would swing high up, held only by its foot. Because of this it is strongly recommended that the trap is not used unless the operator can be concealed nearby, ready to deal with the captive as soon as it is caught.

The foot trap, as seen in Figure 58, depends upon the use of a trip bar placed across an animal track. The snare is looped over the trip bar and its free end is tied to a short piece of wood, which serves as a catch when caught around one of the bar supports. The catch also has another cord fastened around it and this leads to an overhanging bent tree branch. When a long legged animal such as a deer or antelope collides with the trip bar its foot will automatically drop inside the noose and as this is dislodged the wooden catch is released. In turn the branch straightens and the animal is pulled upwards, held by a foot in the now tightened snare. The bar supports are usually concealed, probably with tall grass or bushes and the bar can also be camouflaged, so long as the movement of the drawcord is not impeded.

No doubt human ingenuity could be turned to inventing many other kinds of traps from simple and readily available materials, and a lack of all the requirements for the traps described here could provoke the development of variations. Successful trapping depends as much upon a knowledge of animal habits and behaviour as upon the refinement of traps as machines. Books can supply a certain amount of information concerning the way wild animals live, but there is no substitute for keen observation in the field. A good trapper has to put himself in the place of the animal he is seeking, think like the animal and appreciate the fear it will feel and the caution it will observe when faced with strange and possibly hostile structures. If he is waiting near to a trap, he will need to observe the wind direction and ensure that it blows from the animal towards him and not the reverse. He must remember that other animals can give warning of potential danger to those he is trying to catch. A bird up in a tree can see him, even if his quarry cannot and a warning shriek from the bird will drive the animal away. In the silence of woods and forests sounds will carry for long distances, and movements must be stealthy and quiet, as the snapping of a dry twig by an ungainly boot will rap out like a rifle shot. Trained soldiers, especially those trained as part of a survival unit, should not only be familiar with these tactics, but should also have developed an instinctive knack of noticing the slightest movements which betray anything believing that it is concealed from view.

Suppliers of Traps

United States

Bob-N-Jack Trap, 110 Eighth Street, Farmington, Minnesota, 55024	Pigeon traps
Boyer-Winona Corp, P.O. Box 278, Winona Lake, Ind., 46590	Mouse traps
Campbell Cage Co, Inc, P.O. Box 545, Campbell, California, 95008	Live traps
Hancock Trap Co, 110 S 19th Street, Hot Springs, South Dakota, 57747	Beaver live traps
Havahart, P.O. Box 551, Ossining, New York, 10562	Live cage traps
The Hawkins Co, (Blake & Lamb), Box 175, South Britain, Conn 06487	Blake & Lamb Longspring and over-spring steel traps
King Products, Inc, 4 East Main Street, Gosport, Indiana, 47433	Mouse traps
McGill Metal Products Co, 110 Prairie Street, Marengo, Illinois, 60152	Rodent deadfall traps

Z. A. Macabee Gopher Trap Co, 110 Loma Alta Avenue, Los Gatos, California, 95030	Pocket gopher traps
Nash Mole Traps, RFD1, Scotts, Michigan, 49088	Choker-loop mole traps
National Live Trap Corp, P.O. Box 302, Tomahawk, Wisconsin, 54487	Live traps
Oberto Trap Co, P.O. Box 88, Iron Belt, Wisconsin, 54536	Steel traps
J. R. Schuyler & Co, 152 W. Fourth St, Bloomsburg, Pennsylvania, 17815	Deadfall Traps
Sensitronix, 2225 Lou Ellen, Houston, Texas, 77018	Live traps (birds and mammals)
Shawnee, 3934-A Buena Vista, Dallas, Texas, 75204	Fish trap
H. B. Sherman, P.O. Box 683, De Land, Florida, 32720	Live traps, gophers, rats, mice
Sullivan's Sure Catch Traps, P.O. Box 1241, Valdosta, Georgia, 31602	Live traps
Raymond Thompson Co, 15815 Second Place, W Alderwood Manor, Washington, 98036	Snares
Tomahawk Live Trap Co, P.O. Box 323, Tomahawk, Wisconsin, 54487	Cage traps

Tyler Products, 4525 Fifth Street, Puyallup, Washington, 98371	Diamond jaw mole traps
Woodstream Corp, Animal Trap Div, P.O. Box 327, Lititz, Pa, 17543	Guillotine, scissor mole traps; gopher traps; rat and mouse traps; snares; Victor and Newhouse Steel traps; Conibear traps

Britain

Longworth Scientific Instrument Co, Radley Road, Abingdon, Oxon	Longworth small mammal traps
A.D. Ltd, 170 Almners Road, Lyne, Chertsey, Surrey KT16 0BJ	Auto mouse trap, Cage traps
Gilbertson and Page Ltd, Hertford, Hertfordshire	Juby, Fenn Mark 4, Lloyd, Legg midget, Duffus and pincer mole traps
James Wood Products, Cross Street, Polegate, Sussex	Jamie mink and squirrel trap
Bryants, 16 Ditton Hill Road, Long Ditton, Surrey	Fenn Mark 4, Duffus, Selfset mouse and rat, Auto mouse, Cage traps, Snares

Selfset Ltd, Falcon Works, Hanworth Road, Sunbury, Middlesex	Selfset mouse and rat traps
A. Fenn, High Street, Astwood Bank, Redditch, Worcestershire	Fenn Mark 4
W. Flanagan & Son Ltd, Hanson Road, Aintree, Liverpool	Hunter fox trap
Fuller Engineering Ltd, Three Trees, Loxwood Road, Bucks Green, Rudgwick, Sussex	Legg midget and single catch

France

A. L. Guillouard, Boite Postale 382, Nantes	Klavel lobster pot

Bibliography

Ashcroft, G. & Reese, D. 'An Improved Device for Catching Deer', *Calif Fish & Game* (1957), 43: 193–9

Bateman, James A. *Animal Traps and Trapping* (Newton Abbot, 1971)

Belton, P. & Pucat, A. 'A Comparison of Different Lights in Traps for *Culicoides* (Diptera, Ceratopogonidae)', *Can Ent* (1967), 99: 267–72

Bouskell, James. 'The Cost of Game Preserving', *The Field* (1974), 245:6339: 234–7

Bretherton, R. F. 'Moth Traps and their Lamps: An Attempt at Comparative Analysis', *Entomol Gazette* (1954), V: 145–54

Brown, Ernest R. 'A Compact Lightweight Live Trap for Small Mammals', *J of Mammalogy* (1969), 50:1: 154–5

Burne, B. P. *et al.* 'Collecting, Preparing and Preserving Insects', *Canadian Dep of Agric* (1955), Pub No 932

Casto, William & Presnall, Clifford C. 'Comparison of Coyote Trapping and Methods', *J Wildlife Management* (1944), 8:1: 65–70

Chitty, J. W. & Kempson, D. A. 'Prebaiting Small Mammals and a New Design of a Live Trap', *Ecology* (1949), 30: 536–42

Cox, J. W. 'The Use of Methanal (Formaldehyde Solution) in Pitfall Traps', *Sch Sci Rev* (1975), 55:198: 84–6

Crowcroft, P. & Jeffers. 'Variability in Behaviour of Wild House-mice (*Mus musculus* L) Towards Live Traps', *Proc Zoo Soc Lond* (1961), 137: 573–82

Davies, L. & Williams, C. B. 'Studies on Blackflies (Diptera: Simulidae) Taken in Light Traps in Scotland. I Seasonal Distribution, Sex Ratio and Internal Condition of Catches', *Trans Roy Ent Soc Lond* (1962), 114: 1–20

Davis, D. E. & Emlen, J. T. 'Differential Trappability of Rats According to Age and Size', *J Wildlife Management* (1956), 20: 326–7

Davis, F. M. 'Fishery Gear of England and Wales', *Fish Invest* (1937), Series II, V, No 4

Edgar, R. L. 'A Compact Live Trap for Small Mammals', *J Mammalogy* (1962), 43:4: 547–50

Edwards, E. & Mearney, R. A. 'American Parlour Trap Best', *World Fishing* (1968), 17 (7) 32–3

Eley Game Services. Annual Reports 1962–9 (Fordingbridge)

Fallis, A. M., Bennett, G. F., Griggs, G., & Allen, T. 'Collecting *Simulium venustum* females in Fan Traps and on Silhouettes with the Aid of Carbon Dioxide', *Canadian J Zool* (1970), 45: 1011–17

Fitzwater, William D. 'Trapping an Old Art', *Fish, Fur, Game* (1971), June

Frost, S. W. & Pepper, J. 'Aphids Attracted to Light Traps', *Ann Ent Soc America* (1957), 50: 581–3

Giles, R. *Wildlife Management Techniques*, 3rd Ed (USA, 1969)

Gouldsberg, P. A. (Edit). *Predatory Mammals in Britain*, Council for Nature (1967)

Greenslade, P. J. M. 'Pitfall Trapping as a Method for Studying Carabidae', *J Anim Ecol* (1964), 33: 301–10

Harding, A. R. *The Trapper's Companion*, (revised ed) (USA, 1946)

Harrison, C. J. O., Cowles, G. S., & Dahl, A. C. *Instructions for Collectors, No. 2A Birds*, British Museum (Nat Hist) (1970)

Hollom, P. A. D. 'Trapping Methods for Birds', *BTO Field Guide* No 1 (1950)

Hovell, Mark. *Rats and How to Destroy Them* (1924)

ICI Game Services. Annual Reports 1956–61 (Game Research Station, Fordingbridge)

Karpe, Herman Mŭller. *Handbuch der Vorgeschichte*, Band 1, *Attsteinzeit* (Berlin, 1966)

King, C. M. 'A System for Trapping and Handling Live Weasels in the Field', *J Zool* (1973), 171:4: 458–64

Kleiman, Devra. 'Scent Marking in the Canidae', *Symp Zool Soc London* (1969), 18: 167–77

Luff, M. L. 'Some Effects of Formalin on the Numbers of

Coleoptera Caught in Pitfall Traps', *Entomol Monthly Mag* (1968), 104: 115–6

McCracken, Harold. *How to Catch More Fur* (USA, 1945)

Mangum, C. L. & Callahan, P. S. 'Attraction of Near Infra-red Radiation to *Aedes aegypti*', *J econ Ent* (1968), 61: 36–7

Mead, Chris. *Bird Ringing* (BTO, 1974)

Mossman, A. S. & Reynolds, B. G. R. 'Some African Techniques for Capturing Mammals', *J Mammalogy* (1962), 43:2: 419–20

Munro, Robert. 'Notes on Some Curiously Constructed Wooden Objects Found in Peat Bogs in Various Parts of Europe, Supposed to Have Been Otter and Beaver Traps', *Proc Soc of Ant of Scot* (1891), Vol XXV, 73–89

Munro, Robert & Gillespie, Patrick. 'Further Notes on Ancient Wooden Traps—The So-called Otter & Beaver Traps', *Proc Soc of Ant of Scot* (1919), Vol LIII, Fifth Series, Vol V: 162–7

Netboy, Anthony. *The Atlantic Salmon* (1968)

Novakowski, N. S. *Review of Humane Trapping* (Canada 1970)

Oldroyd, Harold. *Collecting, Preserving and Studying Insects* (1958)

Owen, D. 'Hoverflies in the Garden', *Country Life* (1977), CLXI: 4159: 658–63

Porter, R. F. 'Trapping Songbirds for the Table', *Country Life* (1973), CLIII: 3958: 1206–8

Provost, M. W. 'The Influence of Moonlight on Light-trap Catches of Mosquitoes', *Ann Ent Soc America* (1959), 52: 261–71

Reid, R. W. 'Ancient Wooden Traps from the Moss of Auquharney, Aberdeenshire', *Proc Soc of Ant of Scot* (1922), LVI, Fifth Series, Vol VIII: 282–7

Robinson, H. S. & Robinson, P. J. M. 'Some Notes on the Observed Behaviour of Lepidoptera in Flight in the Vicinity of Light Sources, Together with a Description of a Light Trap Designed to Take Entomological Samples', *Entomol Gazette* (1950), 1: 3–20

Rowe, J. J. 'Grey Squirrel Control', *Forestry Commission Leaflet 56* (1973)

Rowley, W. A. & Jorgenson, N. M. 'Relative Effectiveness of Three Types of Light Traps in Collecting Adult Culicoides', *J econ Ent* (1967), 60: 1478–9

Sanderson, Wilfred E. *Trapping With Havahart Traps* (USA, 1969)

Service, M. W. 'The Use of Insect Suction Traps for Sampling Mosquitoes', *Trans Roy Soc Trop Med & Hyg* (1969), 63:5: 656–63

Service, M. W. 'The Use of Traps in Sampling Mosquito Populations', *Ent exp & appl* (1969), 12: 403–12

Service, M. W. 'A Battery-operated Light Trap for Sampling Mosquito Populations', *Bull Wld Health Org* (1970), 43: 635–41

Sudia, W. D. & Chamberlain, R. W. 'Battery-operated Light Trap, An Improved Model', *Mosquito News* (1962), 22: 126–9

Sullivan, John. 'The Pennsylvania Game Law and You—Traps and Trappers', *Penn Game News* (1958), Dec: 34–7

Varley, M. E. *British Freshwater Fishes* (1967)

Vinter, F. Jean. *Facts About Furs* (USA, 1973)

Index

Page numbers in italics denote illustrations.

A unique how-to-do-it guide to humane and legal trapping of animals, birds, fish, and insects.

JAMES A BATEMAN

TRAPPING

A PRACTICAL GUIDE

James Bateman, known worldwide as an authority on primitive and modern trapping methods, is uniquely qualified to write a practical book on trapping. He has made a life-long study of trapping methods, from Paleolithic foot traps to the latest survival snare designs and live traps. His **Animal Traps and Trapping**, which is the standard work on trapping from an historical viewpoint, has sold over 100,000 copies around the world and now Mr Bateman brings his wide experience into a practical focus in **Trapping: A Practical Guide.**

Mr Bateman knows from experience that each kind of trap has been invented for a specific purpose – from catching food, to controlling pests. In **Trapping: A Practical Guide**, he shows how to select and use the right trapping method for every situation – how to bait, set, and maintain a wide variety of traps for humane and legal trapping of fish, animals, insects, and birds.

Trapping: A Practical Guide is a concise, well-illustrated guide to inexpensive trapping methods anyone – homeowner, farmer, sportsman and naturalist – can use safely. Choose the right trap from over a hundred traps and snares fully described and recommended by an expert who has used them all; then follow his sound advice on specific trapping techniques for a wide variety of creatures including rodents, garden pests, fish, game animals, and birds.

All over the world, trapping is still a reliable way to obtain food and other necessities of life. **Trapping: A Practical Guide** emphasizes the practical value of modern trapping skills, as well as its role as a legitimate survival tool for campers and outdoors enthusiasts. Bateman also recognizes its function as a modern

(Continued on back flap)